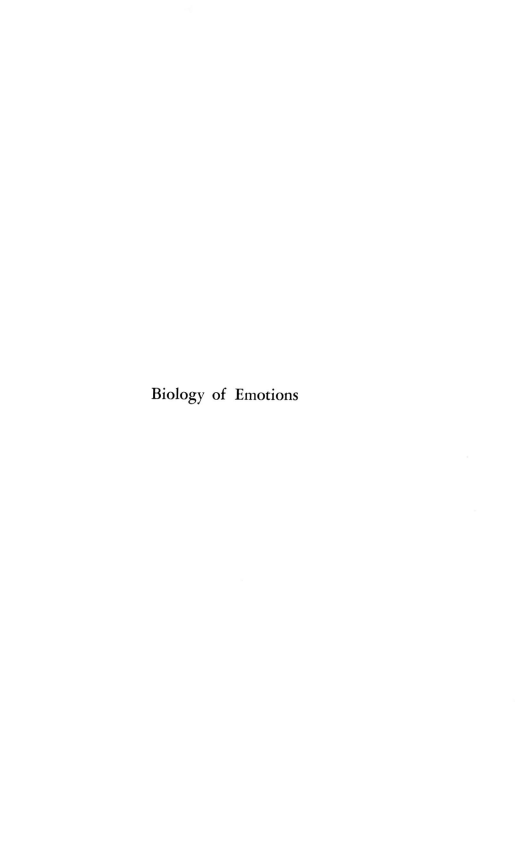

Biology of Emotions

Biology of Emotions

New Understanding Derived from Biological Multidisciplinary
Investigation; First Electrophysiological Measurements

By

EDMUND JACOBSON, M.D., Ph.D., LL.D., F.A.C.P., F.I.C.A.

*Director, Laboratory for Clinical Physiology
and the Jacobson Clinic
Formerly, Assistant Professor of Physiology
University of Chicago
Associate Attending Physician
Michael Reese Hospital
Chicago, Illinois*

CHARLES C THOMAS • PUBLISHER
Springfield • Illinois • U.S.A.

Published and Distributed Throughout the World by
CHARLES C THOMAS • PUBLISHER

BANNERSTONE HOUSE
301-327 East Lawrence Avenue, Springfield, Illinois, U.S.A.
NATCHEZ PLANTATION HOUSE
735 North Atlantic Boulevard, Fort Lauderdale, Florida, U.S.A

© *1967, by* CHARLES C THOMAS • PUBLISHER
Library of Congress Catalog Card Number: 67-12705

With THOMAS BOOKS *careful attention is given to all details of
manufacturing and design. It is the Publisher's desire to present books
that are satisfactory as to their physical qualities and artistic possibilities
and appropriate for their particular use.* THOMAS BOOKS *will be true
to those laws of quality that assure a good name and good will.*

Printed in the United States of America
Q-1

To

MERVIN J. KELLY, Ph.D.

Illustrious in achievements

ACKNOWLEDGMENTS

I am deeply indebted to Richard E. Lange for his technical assistance and skill in taking most of the recordings shown in the figures; and to Helene Roadruck for her counsel and endless patience in preparing the manuscript.

EDMUND JACOBSON

PREFACE

Laboratory and clinical investigations on emotion here to be reviewed have been extensive, covering a span of thirty-five years. Often, observations have been made daily. Possibly this is unique, for in most fields, investigations are not continued interminably but are conducted only for a few years. The net advantage has been an unusually prolonged opportunity for our investigators to observe and to repeat their observations as well as to perform control tests in many variations. Thus, in a veritable lifetime of experience it has become possible to test and to retest, until my own doubts and skepticism have become cautiously dissipated or at least assessed reliably. Another advantage has been the skilled help of many individuals, trained to high competency in autosensory observation, against whose subjective observations simultaneous objective recordings could be checked.

The methods employed have been carefully controlled and multidisciplinary, in the psychological sense as well as the physiological, the subjective as well as the objective, the mathematical as well as the electrical and the therapeutic as well as the purely scientific.

Every methodological approach employed in the present investigations has confirmed the participation of neuromuscular patterns whenever emotion occurs. This finding would be dramatic but for the slight energy costs of these patterns. In each moment of emotion the pattern has been shown to be as specific as the pattern in each moment of locomotion or other muscular act. The muscle contraction commonly is overt, but part of the pattern is always miniscule, requiring electrophysiological registration for confirmation. Miniscule neuromuscular contraction patterns, according to my conclusion, are in part the physiological basis of what in the past has generally been called mental. Thus, we have an empirical basis for the physiology and psychology of emotion.

The methods of autosensory observation which I had developed and had passed on, by training of graduate students and faculty members in psychology at Harvard and Cornell and of subjects in my Chicago laboratory and clinic, resulted in accumulation of extensive data. The reports were independent on the part of the subjects and carefully controlled. The observations of these many subjects led to a significant conclusion: *At any moment of human response, neuromuscular tension patterns along with images constitute the subjectively observable portions of mental activities.* In 1929, I asked myself: Can this be tested objectively? The previous investigations of Golla and others afforded no satisfactory answer. Electromyographs were not available commercially in the twenties. Even today, there is no instrument commercially available for the accurate measurement of the very low voltage transients requisite for the systematic measurement and recording of mental activities. Accordingly, I was confronted with the necessity of devising assemblies myself with the aid of competent advisors on circuit design. An account of this will appear elsewhere.[1]

The results have been widely tested and confirmed by various investigators. In an editorial entitled "Physiological Measurements of Emotional Tension,"[2] Dr. Morris Fishbein quotes from a report in the British Royal Society of Medicine by Dr. Peter Sainsbury of Chichester. Agreeing with Sainsbury, Fishbein writes: "Jacobson was the first to record the action potentials in the muscles and to show that they vary in a predictable way with mental activity and especially with feelings of tension." These early publications, credited as the first to report electrical measurement of mental activities, including emotions, were dated from 1927 to 1930. Since then they have been confirmed repeatedly.[3]

---

[1] JACOBSON, E.: *Physiological Psychiatry*, 1968.
[2] *Postgrad. Med.*, p. 672-674, June 1958.
[3] *Vide infra.*

INTRODUCTION

BLUEPRINT OF EMOTIONS

W HAT IS MAN? This question of ancient writers deserves an answer from modern science. Man is a self-run, self-modifying instrument. However, he has not known this and has much to learn about it.

The instrument is made by nature. It is reproducible through genes and chromosomes, DNA and RNA, with millions of enzymatic and other chemical, physical and electrical processes orderly interwoven. Variation in these or other basic determinants is responsible for individuality.

Through the division of labor among systems in the evolution of man, there occur countless specialized automatic operations which have become the subject matter of the science we call *physiology*. Non-automatic actions are evolved only in and through one system, wherein the striated neuromuscular tissues are the performers. With their circuits in the cerebrospinal nervous system they constitute the anatomic basis of voluntary acts. These acts are what philosophers and laymen have called *will*. We shall call them *effort circuits*.

Through this natural development man has become able to join voluntary efforts for survival and success with automatic reactions in the same direction. This joint action I have called the *welfare response* in man and higher animals. In lower forms, only the automatic reactions are identifiable. With these limitations, the welfare response can be said to be universal to all animals at practically all moments.

These underlying principles lead us to a better understanding of emotions of the whole man and thereafter to a certain measure of control. The motivations of the welfare response, as we shall see, are part and parcel to the physiologic response itself. However, this is true only to the extent that the messages conveyed by a telegraph key are intrinsically part and parcel of the electrical impulses and the clicks involved. To understand the mind of man, we must, for the first time, distinguish between the messages and their meanings. Contrary to current physiological vernacular, the nervous system never really engages in "information processing." We can appreciate this if we realize that the clicks of the telegraph key along with the electrical impulses do not really process information, but only present a code for interpretation.

Thus, from one point of view, the mind of man consists of representative processes or signals comparable with the clicks and electrical impulses of the telegrapher, but which must be interpreted. In other words, we distinguish between representative processes and their meanings, regarding both as different aspects of mental activity. Emotion always includes both representative processes and their meaning to the subject.

Among these signals, certain ones present man's goals to him in their patterned flux. The key to man's emotions and emotional expressions are his goals. He images or otherwise represents what to set out for (in accordance with his welfare impulses). Thus, he has goals or ends which trigger his effort patterns ceaselessly. Often the end is the satisfaction of an urge from his automatic equipment, including hunger, thirst and procreation. Then the voluntary system subserves the involuntary, as Kempf set forth.[4]

Man's emotions vary with hindrances or facilitations, thus pleasantly or unpleasantly. His emotions accordingly may take the form of anger, pursuit, retreat and other so-called passive forms. Emotions of every variety thus become depicted internally in his representations, externally in his behavior, always in relation to his goals. He knows his meanings and often can express them. However, generally he ignores the representative processes or codes which carry these meanings. To learn to recognize them requires prolonged scientific observational training. Lacking this discipline, investigators and doctors will continue like laymen to regard man socially but nontechnically. They will fail to understand his inbuilt devises, as technicians must their computers and *black boxes*. They will continue to miss the whole man.

---

[4] KEMPF, E. J.: *Psychopathology*. St. Louis, Mosby, 1921.

Until these basic principles are recognized, then, the emotions of man and higher animals cannot fully be understood and investigated.

Emotions may be defined as welfare responses marked by total nervous system action in which that of the vegetative system predominates. From this the possibility of partial emotions control by direct scientific methodology becomes apparent. *The avenue of control is through striated muscles, since they alone are the site of volition and of freedom in man.* As we shall see, vegetative nervous system response patterns are inextricably associated with cerebrospinal response patterns, but when either system relaxes, the other tends to relax likewise. Accordingly, the physiology of the control of emotions is opened to investigation and to practical application. The present volume will be devoted to exposition of this thesis and to examples in education and medicine.

SPECIFICATIONS IN THIS MONOGRAPH

As frequently emphasized, the derivation of the word *emotion* suggests a relationship to motion. Even in painting it is recognized that to convey emotion, the painter needs to make some indication of motion. Accordingly, in a broad and general sense we can expect that emotions will have some relation to movements of man and higher animals. Our attention then turns naturally to impulsive actions, for in our daily experience we are impressed with the impulsive aspect of emotions.

Impulsive action, however, appears to comprise a larger class of animal activities. The activities even of microorganisms might belong to this larger class. If so, we can perhaps gain background or context on the impulsive actions of higher animals from a preliminary review of investigations on lower organisms.

A survey of this field is presented in Chapter I. The rationale of the movements of microorganisms for survival leads us to formulate the welfare response, applicable to all animals.

However, eminent physiologists have indicated that impulsive actions can lead further. Claude Bernard, Walter Cannon and J. S. Haldane emphasized the significance of the "free and independent life." This thesis is developed in Chapter II. The indispensible role of the patterned neuromuscular response and the connections in the cerebrospinal nervous system deserves attention. For these activities we shall employ the term *effort circuit* in a sense of this phrase carefully defined.

Animal studies have contributed most to our knowledge of brain circuits involved. These are reviewed in Chapter III. The brilliant contributions of various investigators are noted. However, the results of these investigations lack order and rationale. The animal's subjective states are not revealed by the animal (since this is obviously impossible) nor are they tested by objective methods[5] as will be described herein for man. Animal psychology, indeed, can be called only a "half-science." Even if easier to investigate, *behavior* is not *psyche*.

We shall look to combined objective and subjective investigations of man, therefore, to afford us a fuller science of emotions.

Neglected in the studies of psychologists and psychiatrists has been the internal communication system readily identified in man. This can be understood as the *key to behavior*. Chapter IV outlines this subject. We begin to see integration brought into the rationale of emotions.

Even theories of emotion of the preceding century included the role of voluntary muscles. In present laboratory and clinical investigations, it becomes useful to consider the underlying physiology. For convenience, our terminology turns to effort circuits. We find evidence, partly neglected heretofore, that emotion (even in so-called passive forms) includes an element of effort.

Without question, effort involves neuromuscular and nervous chemical expenditure deriving from breakdown of creatine phosphate, adenosinetriphosphate, etc.[6] Thus every effort costs energy. However, from an entirely different viewpoint, it is true also that the expenditure of this energy is for welfare achievement; in other words, every effort has a goal or more than one. We can assume that the direction is toward accomplishment or end. Accordingly, to the individual the cost may justify the expense.

---

[5] Someday, I trust, this will become scientifically possible.

[6] BOURNE, G. H. (Ed.): *The Structure and Function of Muscle.* Vol. II New York, Academic, 1960, pp. 56-63.

Evidently, the figure of man as a whole begins to loom.

In Chapter VI, we turn back the clock to a previous generation of students of emotion and examine their views. Outstanding scientists contributed. The science of emotion began to evolve in the theories of C. Lange, William James and Walter Cannon. However, in the light of present investigations, these theories are primitive. We shall try to preserve from them what is valuable.

"New principles of mind and brain" based on investigations in our laboratory and clinic are the subject of Chapter VII. We shall see that traditional views of brain and mind never were supported by laboratory evidence yet are current today as if established. These traditional views block a clear understanding of the physiology of emotions.

Since the time of Lange and of James, students generally would shy from attributing emotion to the brain alone. The work of Cannon located significant occurrences in the digestive tract and other viscera. In clinical psychology and medicine I have pursued this theme scientifically and therapeutically. In my experience, emotion subserves the function of evaluation of external environment and of internal conditions (Chapter VIII). Without it human evaluating would be colorless—intellectualistic only. This view is distinctly additional to older conceptions of emotion, whether of Aristotle or of William James or of Walter Cannon. It can help us to understand why in anxiety and other emotional states where the individual engages in prolonged appraisal of real or imagined difficulties, the result can be over-energetic use, or abuse of the visceral structures which engage. The result can be physiological-pathological change. It may or may not be additive to structural changes already initiated by other causes. It may be diagnosed spastic esophagus, irritable colon, peptic ulcer or otherwise. In the cardiovascular system, the pathological condition may be recognized as a form of high blood pressure or exhaustive low pressure or as part of the psychosomatic state associated with angina or coronary disease.

Emotion is shown to be not wholly passive, as many believe, but only partially so. Since emotion includes striated muscle action, it is purposive voluntary action (Chapter VIII) to this limited extent. This is a new view of the functional nature of emotions, really including an element of choice (welfare response). The voluntary element appears not only in active attention, but also in the neuromuscular processes which condition the occurrence of imagery (Chapter IX).

Evidence suggests that physiological processes underlying conscious imagery may often be subthreshold. To this the term *subvisualization* or *residual visualization* is applicable. Analogous considerations and terms apply to other types of imagery.

According to the author's experience, the classification of persons into types of imagery employed is no longer tenable. All persons with normal vision tested in the present studies have been found to employ visual imagery, but this can be extremely vague and transient, requiring technical methods to develop discernment.

The present volume aims chiefly at scientific understanding rather than at methods of clinical or daily control of emotion. However, the individual technically experienced in discerning striated muscle action which characterizes emotion thereby has covered groundwork leading to practical applications toward emotions control. In this sense, the proof of the theoretical pudding lies in the practical successful application. These and the related matters discussed in Chapters X, XI and XII are recapitulated in the final chapter.

NATURE AND FUNCTION OF MIND

It has now become possible to define the mind of man and higher animals, so that its operations are as clearly set forth as are those of circulation, digestion and other systems. The importance of an identifying definition will be obvious to scientists and to clinicians alike.

Definitions, we know, are chiefly of two types. Most people expect a definition to set forth outstanding characteristics, including the very nature of the defined. In this sense, the term *electricity* has not yet become definable.

The other type of definition identifies what is defined by distinguishing marks. In this sense the term *electricity* can be defined accurately and usefully.

The investigations to be outlined in the following pages enable us to offer an identifying definition of mind. It is believed that it will appeal to most scientists and clinicians, possibly including psychologists and psychiatrists of diverse schools.

We shall take into account that every mental operation like that of every other physiological function is energy-consuming at the moment. However, our evidence will indicate that the mental operation can be regarded as the integrated action of the entire nervous-muscular systems in unison, with momentary muscular energy expenditure freed by the breaking of adenosinetriphosphate and other complex phosphate bonds. If we abandon the traditional fears and phobias of the conservative physiologist, we may add that in each mental operation the organism spends energy for a purpose, namely welfare response (Chapters I and II).

In general, then, we assume that each mental operation is an energy expenditure for the purpose of welfare response. Accordingly, we can formulate the principle as follows:

The mind is that energy-expending function of the organism by which it programs its behavior.

In every chapter of this volume, the specific function of emotion will be analyzed from one standpoint or another as a type of mental operation. It will be readily seen that, in emotion, the mental operation is intensified and narrowed in scope of reference to the environment. The energy cost is increased in relation to the importance of the task to which the organism is directed. In critical tasks as in fight or flight, the cost may increase and even become excessive.

CONTENTS

Biology of Emotions

Chapter I
THE WELFARE RESPONSE

The Welfare Response Delineated

AVAILABLE evidence warrants the belief that at any moment of life, every organism, large or small, needs to meet external and internal conditions by appropriate adjustments and adaptations, including the maintenance of a certain homeostasis. This generalization presently accords with the results of countless investigations by biologists in their various fields. The responses are needed for survival and procreation, and in this sense at least they are purposive. They occur in organs, in tissues, in fluids within the organism and in the cells themselves. We shall see that they involve the very elements of the cells.

I here propose that we call these internal and external actions and reactions of organisms their *welfare responses.*

It Includes Homeostasis

The welfare response implies what physiologists have called *free and independent life.* In this connection, we recall that Claude Bernard coined the expression *milieu interne,* in recognition of the blood and the interstitial lymph, providing a vehicle by which nourishment is carried to body cells and waste products are carried away. He pointed out that so long as a certain constancy is maintained in these vehicles, the organism is free from external viscissitudes. In crediting his predecessor for insight into what he later named *homeostasis,* Walter B. Cannon quotes him as follows: "It is the fixity of the *milieu interieur* which is the condition of free and independent life and all the vital mechanisms, however varied they may be, have only one object, that of preserving constant the conditions of life in the internal environment." Following this quotation, Cannon continues: "No

3

more pregnant sentence, in the opinion of J. S. Haldane, 'was ever framed by a physiologist.' "[1]

If thus three great physiologists agree that homeostasis is of obvious importance since it *is the condition of free and independent life,* this very emphasis suggests that we will do well to analyze more clearly the real nature of free and independent life. For the most part, the study of homeostasis takes us into the realm of the vegetative nervous system. Free and independent life, however, is the department chiefly of the cerebrospinal nervous system and the neuromusculature. Obviously, we become involved with automatic procedures when we investigate the functions of the vegetative nervous system. However, the data change in character when we turn to the functions of the cerebrospinal system operating in the intact organism. The integrated operation of these two branches of the nervous system will interest us throughout this volume. Study of the welfare response leads us to consider what physiologists and clinicians generally have preferred to postpone, namely, the study of the organism operating as a whole.

Free and Independent Life

We do not assume that at each moment throughout the organism one and only one response will meet its needs successfully. From what we know, it would seem that variability commonly is permissible. In higher organisms we would call this *choice.* At times, no doubt, the choices that permit successful adaptation may be limited in number, perhaps to one or perhaps even to zero, whereupon there is failure.

The welfare response may be performed by the whole organism or by significant portions thereof. We have need of a term that focuses our attention on the intact organism acting as a whole. We have neglected this and know too little about free and independent life. It is my hope that in biology, as well as in medicine, the use of the term may promote our basic thinking and thus our research.

---

[1] CANNON, W. B.: *The Wisdom of The Body.* New York, Norton, 1960, p. 38.

Emotion Is Implicated in Welfare Response

We can understand emotion better if we recognize that it is implicated in welfare response, as I shall try to show in the contents of this book. If so, our discussion of emotion can appropriately be introduced in a belief preliminary review of various considerations in general physiology, to which we now proceed.

Welfare Response and Energy Balance

Welfare response can usefully apply to action of the animal organism whenever this is normative, adaptive or otherwise favorably functional.[1a] Action commonly will take the form of the performance of work in one sense or another,[2] and we shall see that this applies to emotion. But in any form, whether the nerve supply to the acting part is cerebrospinal, vegetative or both, action affects energy balance.

The energy balance of any organism is kept fairly constant through adjustments of the four important variables: food intake; stored energy; work; and heat production.[3]

We turn now to lower forms of organic life. Recent investigations on unicellular organisms afford grounds for believing that certain of their activities often or commonly can be classed as welfare responses. In a study entitled "Photoresponses of the Fungus, Phycomyces," W. Shropshire, Jr. begins with the com-

---

[1a] Norbert Wiener discusses the "fundamental discovery of thermodynamics," namely, that "the only available source of mechanical energy is the cooling of a hot body and the consequent heating of a cool one." "From this exclusion principle," he comments, "it is possible to set up the entire system which has governed the development of the thermal engine" (Time, communication and the nervous system in teleological mechanisms. *Ann. N.Y. Acad. Sci.* 50:200, Oct. 13, 1948). I doubt that we should try to extend his remarks to apply to what are called *mechanical actions* in living organisms.

[2] Physiologists sometimes use the term *work* not only in the sense of the physicists (force times distance) but also in an additional sense, meaning energy expenditure even if no distance is covered but the expenditure takes place as a time function. For example, steady contraction in muscle is an illustration of physiological work in the latter sense. In either meaning, work in higher organisms occurs chiefly as a specialized function of muscle. Mead believes that the frequency of breathing is adjusted not to minimize work but rather the mean inspiratory muscle force (MEAD, J.: Control of respiratory frequency. *J. Appl. Physiol.*, 15:325-337, 1960).

[3] ANAND, B. K.: Nervous regulation of food intake. *Physiol. Rev. 41*(4):677, 1961.

ment: "One of the central problems of biology, and more specifically of sensory physiology, is the achievement of a complete, precise description of the mechanisms by which the information content of external stimuli is transduced into meaningful responses by an organism."[3a] In his conclusion, the author indicates that only the initial phases of characterization of the responses to light by Phycomyces sporangiophores have been completed. However, he adds that his results are encouraging that such a relatively simple unicellular system is profitable for attacking the sequential mechanism underlying stimulus-response systems. Evidently, the author's studies throw light upon primitive antecedents of what in higher organisms are called *perception* and *interpretation*.

Other studies on amoebae of present bearing have been published recently. J. M. Marshall, Jr., *et al.* report concerning pinocytosis in amoebae. This drinking response can be induced by a variety of salts, proteins and proteinaceous materials. The authors find that protein uptake by pinocytosis proceeds in definite stages, and they cite similar conclusions by other investigators.[4] H. Holter regards pinocytosis as "one of the fundamental processes in the physiology of ameoboid cells."[5] Obviously, pinocytosis, like locomotion in ameobae,[6] is to be regarded as primitive motor rather than as primitive perceptual response in these organisms.

According to J. V. Landau: "It is a well-established fact that all cells at some stage in their physiological activity perform work as a result of the utilization of mechanical energy." Considering locomotion, the same author points out that the plasmagel is constantly exerting a force on the plasmasol, and accordingly pseudopodial flow should follow the path of least resistance. Significantly, Landau concludes: "The existence of a dynamic equi-

[3a] Shropshire, W., Jr.: *Physiol. Rev.*, 43(1):38, 1963.

[4] Marshall, J. M., Jr., Schumaker, V. N., and Brandt, P. W..: Pinocytosis in amoebae, *Ann. N. Y. Acad. Sci.*, 78(2):515-523, June 18, 1959.

[5] Holter, H.: Problems of pinocytosis with special regard to amoebae. *Ann. N. Y. Acad. Sci.*, 78(2):524-537, June 18, 1959.

[6] Landau, J. V.: Sol-gel transformations in amoebae, *Ann. N. Y. Acad. Sci.*, 78(2):487-499, June 18, 1959.

librium between a sol, or fluid state, and a gel, or more highly organized structural state, within the cytoplasm of the amoeba provides the organism with what is probably the most elemental or basic means for the conversion of chemical energy into mechanical work. It is the inherent contractility of this gel state that provides the mechanical force necessary for locomotion, division, excretion, and all other functions of the living organism that are based upon the motility of the cytoplasm."[7]

It is of interest that in unicellular organisms investigators already have been able to identify primitive antecedents of perception differentiable from locomotion, pinocytosis and other motor procedures. We shall have occasion in higher organisms to identify a procedure which I shall term *evaluation*, which is less readily identifiable in the primitive forms of welfare response seen in unicellular organisms.

In the motor responses of higher organisms, chemical studies have turned attention to the role of the hydrolysis of adenosine triphosphate. According to A. M. Zimmerman: "The investigations of adenosine triphosphate tend to suggest that this agent may be the energy source for sol-gel transformations in amoebae. All available data suggest that the formation of a gel structure in protoplasm involves the bonding of certain protein components into a three-dimensional network and that the transition from sol to gel is an endothermic process involving a positive volume change. It is postulated, therefore, that the gelation reaction received energy from the hydrolysis of adenosine triphosphate."[8]

According to H. I. Hirshfield, cytoplasmic activities in the cell of amoeba are to a significant extent under nuclear control. "The available evidence," he states, "leaves little doubt as to the primary role of the nucleus in the following cytoplasmic activities: phosphate turnover, protein gel-sol transformations, and RNA levels."[9] However, whatever the function of the so-called neuro-

[7] *Ibid.*, p. 498.

[8] ZIMMERMAN, A. M.: Effects of selected chemical agents on amoebae. *Ann. N. Y. Acad. Sci.*, 78(2):643, June 18, 1959.

[9] HIRSHFIELD, H. I.: Nuclear control of cytoplasmic activities. *Ann. N. Y. Acad. Sci.*, 78(2):651, June 18, 1959.

motor system of ciliate protozoans may be, C. L. Prosser warns us against assuming that this is a precursor of nervous systems in higher organisms. Rather, he points out, in protozoan cells, as in other cells, excitation of the surface appear to be transmitted from one region to another and to influence internal mechanisms of motion. In contrast, he emphasizes, nervous function takes its origin in the general polarized properties of cell membranes. He adds that it is probable in all cells where ionic gradients exist between the inside and outside there are transmembrane potentials, and, on appropriate stimulation, changes in ion permeability occur. Other bases for excitability exist, such as direct effects of stimuli on contractile proteins or on specific intracellular enzymes. However, that common cellular function which gave rise to nervous conduction, the rapid transmission of signals from one part of an animal to another, seems to reside in cell membranes which can be partially or completely depolarized by chemical, mechanical, thermal or electrical stimulation.[10]

Prosser adds significantly: "A nervous system gives an animal some independence of its environment."[11]

Purpose

E. W. Sinnott discusses "a common basis for development and behavior in organisms." From Bergson he quotes: "Neither mobility nor choice nor consciousness involves as a necessary condition the presence of a nervous system. The latter has only canalized in a definite direction and brought up to a higher degree of intensity a rudimentary and vague activity diffused throughout the mass of the organized substance." Sinnott be-

---

[10] PROSSER, C. LADD,: Comparative neurophysiology. In Bass, A. D.: *Evolution of Nervous Control from Primitive Organisms to Man.* Washington, D. C., A.A.A.S., Publication #52, 1959, pp. 31, 32, 33.

[11] *Loc. cit.* p. 33. Prosser notes that many examples are known of non-nervous conduction from cell to cell. Embryonic muscles, for example, the myotomes of fish embryos, show coordination before they are innervated. On p. 32, Prosser's comment leads us to recall the studies of Weiss on salamanders, in which a fifth leg showed coordinated motility before the ingress of supplying nervous fibers.

lieves that the fact of biological organization as thus emphasized by Bergson is the basis of the control of all vital activities. "It produces the *organism* [italics his], a distinctive feature of life."

"Two facts about organic development," Sinnott adds, "are particularly important: first, it moves toward a precise end, the completed structure or the mature organism. This is familiar to students of embryology. . . . Second, if this normal development is blocked, the organism tends to restore it by processes of self-regulation. Regeneration is a familiar phenomenon. A single isolated blastomere may produce a whole individual. . . . It is as though the whole organism, in a sense, was present in each cell as it is in the egg."

Sinnott concludes that "development seems to be essentially teleological and organism a teleological concept. This implies no 'final' causation, but simply self-regulation to a norm or end. The self-regulation evident in developmental processes," he goes on to say, "is paralleled by the regulatory character of most physiological ones, as evident in the countless cases of homeostasis. It is difficult to make a sharp separation between these more strictly biological processes of embryology and physiology and those psychological ones called behavior. All three are manifestations of the regulatory action of protoplasm: embryology, in the orderly construction and repair of the bodily organism, moving toward a specific norm; physiology, the control of processes taking place within the organism in conformity to a functional norm; and behavior, the regulatory activities of the organism as a whole. Instincts, the simplest sort of behavioral controls, are directed toward specific goals, which change as conditions change."

Sinnott agrees with W. E. Agar; namely, "the chief objective indication of purposiveness in the behavior of living organisms is the familiar fact that the sequence of acts by which the goal is attained is not always the same. On different occasions, the organism reaches the same end by different routes. It must fit the details of its action to the special situation. The completed nest, the spider's web, the act of mating, is attained by a train of acts different in detail on every occasion. It is the end, the purpose, which is important. This remains constant, but is not reached by any single, linear path."[12]

"It is evident," Sinnott continues, "that in all animals above the simplest ones this self-regulatory character is canalized in the highly differentiated nervous system. This makes possible a far more complex behavioral control and thus a far more specialized behavior than where this control is centered in cells which have many other functions. The study of behavior has therefore become chiefly a study of the activities of the nervous system. We should remember, however, that this control is a specialized case of a generalized quality of all living stuff which directs the growth, functioning and behavior of the organism in conformity to norms within it."

Sinnott goes on to offer a theory of mind as follows: "If a behavioral norm, set up in the nervous system, is a primitive purpose and thus a psychical phenomenon, this idea has important implications, for it suggests how a mental act may be related to a bodily one. Mind may thus be regarded as the control of behavior in conformity to norms or purposes set up in the organism." We can agree with this only if we provide that he views mind as purpose in body actions. However, he leaves me far behind when he states: "A conscious purpose is the subjective *experience* [italics his] of this regulation, but primitive purposes are presumably unconscious." I am reminded of the teaching of Professor W. Locy in my first course in elementary zoology: "There is no way to know whether a paramecium is conscious or not short of becoming a paramecium yourself." Accordingly, for the present monograph, we shall leave the question of consciousness in unicellular organisms on a speculative shelf. However, as we shall see, mental operations can be studied electrophysiologically, and with the aid of oscilloscopes their patterns can be seen and followed. Accordingly we have become able to identify certain aspects of emotions as they occur. This will not be speculation, for we will be dealing with human subjects from

---

[12] SINNOTT, E. W.: A common basis for development and behavior in organisms. In Bass, A. D.: *Evolution of Nervous Control from Primitive Organisms to Man.* Washington, D. C., A.A.A.S., Publication #52, 1959, pp. 1-5.

whom we can secure technical subjective reports on their conscious patterns.

Endocrine and Nervous Participation in Emotional Welfare Responses

In the present chapter we can do little more than mark out some of the highlights, the more important features of the welfare response in various stages of animal development. Throughout the discussion of emotions, we shall have need to refer to the endocrine system as well as to the nervous system. In this connection, G. B. Koelle, in a chapter entitled "Neurohumoral Agents As a Mechanism of Nervous Integration" points out: "In the overall regulation of homeostasis, the nervous system controls rapid adjustments to change in the environment, whereas the endocrine system is responsible for slower, more general adaptations. Important segments of both systems are linked at the hypothalamic level so that a major part, if not the entireties, of the nervous and endocrine systems are functionally integrated." "In 1948," Koelle continues, "von Euler[13] presented conclusive evidence that norepinephrine is the predominant, if not the exclusive, transmitter of most adrenergic or postganglionic sympathetic fibers." Euler's discovery has led to modification of the theory of Cannon and Rosenblueth[14] that the sympathetic nervous system and the embryologically related adrenal medulla function as a unit in emergency situations to prepare the organism for fight or flight. It is agreed that the sympathetic nervous system liberates norepinephrine at appropriate and relatively selective sites, thereby regulating the tone of the blood vessels and of other autonomic effectors to adjust to continual changes in posture, activity and environment.[15] Adaptation to emergencies is probably the chief function of the adrenal medulla, which liberates chiefly epinephrine into

---

[13] EULER, U. S. v.: Identification of the sympathomimetic ergone in adrenergic nerves of cattle (sympathin N) with laevo-noradrenaline. *Acta Physiol. Scand.,* 16:63-74, 1948.

[14] CANNON, W. B., and ROSENBLUETH, A.: Autonomic Neuro-Effector Systems. New York, Macmillan, 1937.

[15] CELANDER, O.: The range of control exercised by the "sympatheticoadrenal system." *Acta Physiol. Scand.,* 32 (Suppl. 116):1-132, 1954.

the blood stream. The actions of the two amines are qualitatively similar. However, norepinephrine is more active as a vasoconstrictor and excitor of smooth muscle in general. Epinephrine, however, is more effective as a cardioaccelerator, smooth muscle inhibitor, stimulant to the central nervous system and accelerator of certain metabolic processes, including glycogenolysis and oxygen uptake.[16] Grundfest[17] advances reasons for believing that chemical transmission occurs at all central as well as at all peripheral synapses. Koelle discusses the evidence for assuming that adenosine triphosphate in varying concentrations participate in different regions of the central nervous system as well as its release in muscle following excitation.

Emotion and endocrine activity ordinarily are thought of as two different sets of phenomena. From the studies of Gellhorn and others, it becomes clear that they are really part of the same bodily response considered from two different angles. We necessarily must distinguish and classify according to our specialist points of view. However, nature embodies both in one whole welfare response.

For illustration, I quote from studies by Endröczi and Lissák on cats and dogs where certain characteristic gross behavioral responses were observed with indications that sexual behavior and rage reactions were correlated with the secretory patterns. Their studies are reviewed by R. E. Smith and D. J. Hoijer in an article entitled "Metabolism and Cellular Function in Cold Acclimation."[18] The reviewers discuss adrenal corticotrophic regulation, a subject of importance in endocrinology as well as in the study of emotions. They state that the authors mentioned have clearly indicated the operation of corticoid secretory controls at two levels of the central nervous system, i.e., (a) a fairly direct pathway from reticular formation of the brain stem to the hypothalamus, stimulation of which resembles ACTH activation in augmenting outputs of hydrocortisone and corticosteroids; (b) at a higher level of neuronal control, secretion of the latter two

[16] EULER, U. S. v.: *Noradrenaline, Chemistry, Physiology, Pharmacology and Clinical Aspects.* Springfield, Thomas, 1956.

[17] GRUNDFEST, H.: General problems of drug actions on bioelectric phenomena. *Ann. N. Y. Acad. Sci.,* 66:573-591, 1957.

[18] *Physiol. Rev.,* 42:1, 78, Jan., 1962.

steroids was significantly increased by stimulation of centers in the archicortex (amygdaloid nucleus and pyriform cortex) of both cat and dog, but abolished upon hippocampal stimulation, with attending reduction in output of both compound F and B and some rise in the ratio of F/B.[19]

From the studies mentioned and others, the reviewers conclude that the control mechanism in the intact animal would appear to be a resultant of combinations of neurogenic and systemic inputs. These affect the hypothalamus where a humoral transport system proceeds to the adenohypophysis, in which a complicated interrelationship occurs with production of ACTH.

The reviewers find it pertinent to cite evidence that catechol amines are excitatory to the brain-stem, while negative feedback is evidently achieved through adrenergic inhibition of synaptic transmission through the sympathetic ganglia.[20, 21]

Since cold acclimation is an example of welfare response in the presence of a particular type of stress, we can pertinently note that ascorbic acid has a protective action in acute cold.[22] Cold exposure likewise stimulates synthesis of cholesterol[23] which in turn is a basic precursor of the corticosteroids.[24]

---

[19] ENDRÖCZI, E., and LISSÁK, K.: The role of the mesencephalon, diencephalon and archicortex in the activation and inhibition of the pituitary-adrenocortical system. *Acta Physiol. Acad. Sci. Hung., 17*:39, 1960; ENDRÖCZI, E., LISSÁK, K., BOHUS, B., and KOVACS, S.: The inhibitory influence of archicortical structures on pituitary-adrenal function. *Acta Physiol. Acad. Sci. Hung., 16*:17, 1959.; LISSÁK, K., and ENDRÖCZI, E.: *Die neuroendokrine Steuerung der Adaptationstätigkeit.* Budapest, Verlag der Ungarschen Akademie der Wissenschaften, 1960.

[20] See also FULTON, J. F.: *Physiology of the Nervous System.* New York, Oxford U. P., 3rd ed. 1949.

[21] CLARK, I.: The effect of cortisone upon protein synthesis, *J. Biol. Chem., 200*:69, 1953.

[22] WOLSTENHOLME, G. E. W., and MILLAR, E. C. P. (Eds.): *Ciba Foundation Colloquia on Endocrinology,* Vol. 10, *Regulation and Mode of Action of Thyroid Hormones.* Boston, Little, 1957; *Ciba Foundation Symposium on the Regulation of Cell Metabolism,* London, J and A Churchill, 1959.

[23] MEFFERD, R. B., JR., NYMAN, M. A., and WEBSTER, W. W.: Whole-body lipid metabolism of rats after chronic exposure to adverse environments. *Amer. J. Physiol., 195*:744, 1958. Vahouny, G. V., Flick, D. F., Gregorian, H. M., and Treadwell, C. R.: Nutrition studies in the cold. III. Effects of cold environment on "cholesterol" fatty livers. *J. Nutr. 68*:495, 1959.

[24] SOBEL, H., SIDEMAN, M., and ARCE, R.: Steroid excretion by guinea pigs exposed to cold for prolonged periods. *Amer. J. Physiol., 198*:1107, 1960.

Behavior and Conditioned Reflexes

We return now to the welfare response in so far as illustrated by behavioral acts of the entire organism. In former years, Russian investigators generally tended to try to reduce behavioral acts to patterns of conditioned and unconditioned reflexes. Apparently this fashion is at least beginning to pass away in Russia. Investigators there apparently are realizing that integration by the nervous system surpasses mere combinations of conditioned and unconditioned reflexes. I quote from *Animal Behavior* by L. V. Krushinski[25]: "When passing from the study of the laws of reflex activity to the study of the laws of behavior itself, however, it is impossible to make such a strict division into conditioned and unconditioned reflexes. Behavioral acts in most cases appear to be the result of the complex integration of conditioned and unconditioned reflexes which are mingled into single integral actions. This becomes obvious as soon as the investigator passes from the study of the animal in the laboratory to experimental conditions more natural for the animal."

Later the author adds: "It seems indisputable to us that in the struggle for existence the important factor is not how a particular behavioral act is carried out, but what contribution it ultimately makes toward the survival of the species. This is the main reason why in evolution, as elements of behavior, reactions were formed which were directed toward the execution of definite, biologically useful acts."

Behavior is Integrated Action

Still later the author adds, in summary:

The reflex is the simplest integrated unit of activity of the nervous system. The unitary reaction is the simplest integrated unit of behavior.

The conditioned reflex is a temporary nervous connection, whereas the unconditioned reflex is permanent. The unitary reaction is a combination of temporary and permanent connections into a single behavioral act.

---

[25] Translated by Basil Haigh, M.A., M.B., B. Chir., Consultants Bureau, New York.

The reflex is carried out in accordance with a definite pattern from beginning to end. The unitary reaction of behavior is characterized by a definite pattern of execution only of its final stage. . . .

The unitary reaction may thus be defined as: "an integrated behavioral act formed as a result of the integration of conditioned and unconditioned reflexes, the relaxative proportions of which are not strictly fixed." This behavioral act is directed toward the execution of a single and appropriate action which, although performed by different methods, has a definite pattern of final execution.

The biological form of behavior may thus be defined as: multiaction behavior constructed from individual unitary reactions, associated with the satisfaction of the more important biological requirements of the animal."

In our present terminology the term applied would be *welfare response*. The author emphasizes that in the investigation described it was quite clearly shown "that in the formation of properties of behavior such as defensive reactions, hereditary factors play a very important role." Later the author is careful to quote Pavlov to the effect that the behavior of man and animals is determined not only by the natural properties of the nervous system, but also by those influences which have befallen and are continuing to befall the organism during its individual existence, i.e., it depends on constant training or education in the widest sense of these words.[26]

The welfare response in biology evidently has myriads of aspects, which to delineate only would require many volumes rather than a single chapter. Necessarily, our present purposes limit the scope of this delineation. It is believed, however, that the current literature on emotion as well as that on the autonomic nervous sysem and its functions can be better integrated by the nervous systems of the readers if they will keep this basic conception in mind.

---

[26] Pavlov, I. P.: *Twenty Years' Experience of the Objective Study of the Higher Nervous Activity (Behavior) of Animals.* Biomedgiz, Moscow-Leningrad, 1938, p. 653.

Behavior Science Versus *Introspection*

What is presently known as behavioral sciences has grown to be a vast and important section of biology today. It is interesting, however, to try to trace the beginnings of this development. These are commonly attributed to John B. Watson, who despaired of securing reliable data by self-observation from subjects used in psychological laboratories. Karl Lashley was associated in this endeavor to develop the beginnings of behavioral science. However, years later he said he began to doubt that the assumptions on which he and Watson had been progressing really were free from introspective methodology. In a personal communication to the author, with some amusement he related that he and Watson would spend an evening together drawing conclusions which were really in part based on their own introspections, but without their clearly realizing it at the time.

After the publication of the author's articles on electrical measurement of neuromuscular states during mental activities, in the early 1930s, I was informed that Watson held that my findings, especially those on inner speech, supported his views. However, this support cannot be said to be substantiated. These measurements were certainly objective; nevertheless they were originally suggested by autosensory observations. According to my experience, skill and reliability in autosensory observation needs to be cultivated just as is necessary, for example, with microscopic slides in human pathology. All the evidence indicates that Watson had never been trained sufficiently in autosensory observation.

Nevertheless, it is certain that the efforts of Watson helped to initiate the building of an imposing edifice of the behavioral sciences. What is especially interesting is that this was accomplished on the basis of denying the existence of possible development of autosensory observation, although Watson did not use this term. This is not the first time in science, however, that great positive achievements have resulted following unwarranted denials of other departments of thought. We can explain the positive achievement as resulting from an increased attention and investigation devotion to a circumscribed field, freed from consideration of other fields, however closely related.

I believe that behaviorists in their studies of emotion on animals, and also on man when scientific subjective reports under controlled conditions from trained observers are omitted, deal with only half a science. To understand fully the emotions of animals is not possible for human beings, because of the lack of means of communication. With human beings, however, understanding is wide open, provided the investigator has become sufficiently skilled in subjective techniques to control them and to employ them with what scientic accuracy is available in the subjective field.

We shall see that there are circumstances under which welfare responses can be carried beyond the point of prosperous survival. In the field of emotion, to which this volume is devoted, anxious reflection is an outstanding example in this present "age of anxiety."

Chapter II
THE FREE AND INDEPENDENT LIFE

Life is a function of motion, for complete stasis is death. Animals enjoy a freedom of which plants are bereft. This derives from their capability to move from noxious toward more favorable stimuli, from enemies toward friends and parents —in short, to choose between fight and flight. The capability to move parts as well as the whole also conditions procreation in higher organisms. However, as we have seen, even the lowly amoeba can move in pseudopodia.

Thus, through and by motion, animals on every scale engage in welfare responses over time. We might question whether each and every motion in the organism is determined by conditions which precede and accompany it. The view prevails that causality applies to the inanimate objects in our environment. We can recall David Hume's famous billiard balls. However, looking beyond Hume and his still more famous successor, Immanuel Kant, I here suggest that causality is our way of classifying changes in those objects; it is one interpretation of such changes; but more than our operation in thinking of them. Like any other human operation of understanding, it may be true or false. Indeed, certain physicists do not believe that causality applies to the motions of very small particles, but that chance plays a role.

In classifying the acts of man and of higher animals, we are accustomed to speak of their ability to choose a line of action. Some speculators have believed that any change in any part in and of the organism is but a link in a fantastically intricate chain of causes, but of course it is not possible to test or to prove this. Common experience does not lead us to accept this belief unequivocally, but instead we habitually regard higher animals as capable of free choice. In other words, we believe that the organism determines its own direction. Evidently, even our terminology suggests that the ability to make this determination is centered more in the cerebrospinal section of the nervous system than in the vegetative. In the process of evolution, division of labor has resulted in specialization of motion of higher organisms and their chief parts in one tissue. This is muscle. Internal communication is left chiefly to nervous tissue. However (as I shall point out in Chapter IV), we are not realistic when we assume that the nervous system acts for communication alone after the fashion of telephone wires and central. Instead, at Setschenow and Sherrington saw early in the day, every portion of the brain is connected directly or indirectly with muscle. When nerves act, peripheral organs act, and this includes power, which resides in muscle. "Information processing" in the nervous system —this and no more—a topic on which symposia are held by learned societies—is a figment of the student's imagination. No *black box;* no computer really imitates the nervous system truly (even those that win at checkers) unless muscular power is included.

In the intact organism nervous response is not found to occur unattended by muscular action, unless the nerve is dissected and removed from the organism.

Since muscle is what moves the animal and its chief parts, here lies the final common path of what we know as choice—the *sine qua non* of the free and independent life. Perhaps this is so obvious that we have failed to realize it. Accordingly, in teaching operational physiology, I often request the pupil to engage in some simple act such as bending back his left hand. Thereupon I point out that this skeletal muscle act can serve as a sample of all his efforts. Obviously, *this is you doing something and for a purpose.* To impress the point I may add that *this is a discovery,* in the sense that the act is free and independent, like any other free and independent act he may make. From this point of view efforts will be discussed further in Chapter V.

The freedom and independence of the higher organism to act for welfare resides, then, to a certain extent in muscle and its innervation. If the muscular system is paralyzed, as by curare or like preparations, there occurs no welfare response of fight, flight or procreation.

In man, particularly in subjects experienced in autosensory observation and report, we can examine the welfare response both subjectively and objectively. Clinical experience has led me to classify it as consisting of four functions intricately interrelated. I shall consider them successively, but it is important to warn that they do not occur one after the other in the order named, but, instead, they occur approximately more or less simultaneously, each inseparable from the other three.

Such intricate inseparability of functions should be a familiar theme to the physiologist, for he is accustomed to speak of the circulatory or other systems, well knowing that in the intact animal each and every system does not exist apart but only as an abstraction made in the interests of apprehension and teaching.

The welfare response presents a fuller development in man than in lower organisms. Human activities are more readily interpreted and classified. When in doubt we can ask him about what he is doing and why, and in some instances we can thus learn. These advantages lead us to try to seek understanding of the welfare response in man and later, if desired, to examine lower forms to see if the principles apply in more primitive fashion. Clinical and other experience leads me to classify the human welfare response in four categories, namely, perception, evaluation, reflection and neuromuscular action.

Perception (the Interpretive Response to Signals)

Classically, recalling John Locke, we speak of the senses as basic to perception. However, modern inventive progress leads us to regard living organisms as complex instruments. *This point of view, I believe, will help us to understand man as we have never understood him before.*

Signals from without or from within

Signals triggered from without afford necessary information about external reality. Signals triggered from within afford necessary information about internal conditions.

The signals, or the impulses which convey them, may be perceived or not. Stereotyped actions which occur promptly, directly and predictably following certain types of signal-impulses are known as reflexes. In such cases, perception of the action may not precede it, but may follow.

We need to define what we mean by *perception.* In a study designed toward this end, I found that sensory signals by themselves do not constitute perception. Something more is required. Neuromuscular activity is added to the sensory signals when we perceive an object. A neuromuscular activity occurs which *designates* the sensory signals and this total sensorimotor act is what occurs when we perceive.[1]

For illustration, a printed word is exposed before a subject who has been trained in precise reporting. The visual impressions alone prove insufficient for him to perceive the print as a word with meaning. If he stares at the print, following the method of Gamble, the word and its meaning soon are lost and he sees only print, no matter how simple the meaning and no matter how familiar the word. For example, assume that the word is *boy* and that the subject is educated and speaks and reads English. The word, as such, and the meaning wane and disappear, to reappear when and only when he tenses the muscles of inner speech to say the word and tenses his eye muscles to see something that to him looks like or stands for *boy.*

Authors differ in their usage of the terms *sensation* and *perception.* Some regard them as synonymous. The matter is complicated because electrophysiological investigations indicate that sensation can no longer be regarded as simply the subjective aspect of afferent neuronic action.

> It is clearly established that, whatever may be contributed by upward-streaming sensory-evoked impulses, the central nervous system possesses an important downstream sensory control mechanism which also undoubtedly contributes to the perceptual content.[2]

---

[1] JACOBSON, E.: On meaning and understanding. *Amer. J. Psychol.,* 22:553-577, Oct., 1911.

[2] LIVINGSTON, ROBERT B.: Central control of receptors and sensory transmission systems. In *Handbook of Physiology, Neurophysiology* I. Washington, D. C., American Physiological Society, 1959, Chapter XXXI, pp. 756-757.

However, whatever else takes place in modification, sensation depends primarily upon specific afferent impulses. Admittedly, sensation as unmodified afferent impulses does not occur; nevertheless, it is a convenient abstraction or concept. As such we shall continue to use the term in this manuscript.

According to the investigations cited, we require a term other than *sensation* to distinguish what occurs in man when the experience afforded in one sense is designated in another, particularly wth neuromuscular participation. In the present text, *perception* will mean sensation subjected to neuromuscular designation.

As electronic experts say when they examine a complex circuit, what the circuit from a certain point *sees* explains what takes place. So we might say, also speaking figuratively, that the neuromuscular indicator *sees* the sensory configuration. We should add that just how it looks upon the sensory configuration is a function not only of that configuration but also of the neuromuscular pattern at the moment when it designates. *It follows, as I have found, that if the neuromuscular patterns are sufficiently relaxed, perception wanes toward absence. However, as we shall see, emotion is triggered by perception. Consequently, with the waning of perception, emotion likewise dwindles.*

What has residual tension in man to do with perception, if anything? It has *everything* to do with perception, according to my understanding. By residual tension I mean the neuromuscular activities (and the attendant central ones) which remain over after one experience and which accordingly condition the reception and response to a following experience. The time lapses between one and the other experience generally are on the order of seconds, minutes or hours. What one has been doing largely determines what one continues to do, for there is *momentum* in our perceptive acts as there is momentum everywhere else where particles move.

Residual tension and residual imaging apply to emotions. This explains why a mood, excited by one experience, tends to be carried over into the next, even if irrelevantly.

Residual tension and residual imagery prepare us for immediately oncoming events. So the prizefighter, so the golfer, so the musician, so the businessman prepares and is prepared for what may follow. So we can finish a sentence which we begin to utter or to read, and so we can listen to others or follow a tune.

The significance of residual tension for each moment of living can be illustrated in the act of walking across a city street in danger from approaching vehicles. If suddenly, when crossing the street, the pedestrian were to lose residual tension and imagery completely, he would not for the instant know where he had been, what he was now doing or what he intended to do. In sum, *residual tension plus imagery is the continuance of past awareness and action, the key to orientative present and to programming for the future.*

Memory of the past likewise serves to prepare us for the future; but memory is potential preparation, whereas residual tension plus imaging are not potential but actual present energy expenditure.

Varieties of Perception

On this basis we can better understand overemotionality and nervousness. In both there is excess of effort preparation. When excessive, residual or persevering tension and imagery patterns overshoot the mark. In preparing to meet the future, the individual then works too hard or works too little. What he should seek is the optimum requisite for maximum efficiency.

At any instant he never perceives the whole of reality but only a small portion of it. Vision, the most important of our senses, is an example. He does not see over the whole range of the light spectrum but only over a small portion. Light waves must be within the range of three to seven million millimicrons, else the rods and cones of his retinae will not respond. Thus the range of his visual signals is limited.

There are other limitations. Light signals fail to penetrate opaque bodies which intervene in the path of light rays toward our eyes. There are illusions studied by psychologists. There is the Doppler effect and many other effects on light rays before they reach our retinae. I need not recount the many discoveries of physicists who have specialized in these fields.

To understand visual perception, however, we must go beyond the physics of light. Psychologists long have taught that what

we perceive depends in part upon past experience. The American Indian first to see a gun presumably did not have the same perception of it as did its white owner. Automobiles in this country were first perceived as horseless carriages (and I well remember the day), rather than as examples of General Motors, Fords, Chryslers and foreign cars as occurs today. The point is so obvious that I will not belabor it with further examples. Wilhelm Wundt, "the father of experimental psychology," appreciated the importance of past experience. Accordingly, he labelled our full perceptions *apperception*. However, in his day, residual tension and residual imagery in the present sense were not yet discovered.

Our present aim is limited to bringing out certain relations of perception to emotion, which have not been clearly recognized heretofore. The necessity of further investigation for test and possible corroboration will be evident. To avert misunderstanding, however, we add that it lies beyond the scope and purposes of this manuscript to present even a summary of the principal findings and conclusions of countless investigators whose efforts have built a science of psychophysics and perception. An excellent review to which the interested reader is referred has been published recently under the authorship of Hans-Lukas Teuber.[3]

In one portion of his conclusion, this author states: "Nor can we expect to understand the essential central correlates of perceiving by adhering to those conceptions of the nervous system which view it as a passive receiver of sensory information. The nervous system must operate upon its inputs, not only by selecting them, but by providing the essential 'constancies' without which the information would be chaotic."[4]

To this conclusion we can add the following generalization: *The perception of each individual is within limits determined*

---

[3] Perception. In *Handbook of Physiology, Neurophysiology*, Vol. III. Washington, D. C., Amer. Physiol. Soc., 1960, pp. 1595-1668.

[4] *Loc. cit.*, p. 1660; see also GRANIT, R.: *Receptors and Sensory Perception.* New Haven, Yale, 1955; GIBSON, J. J.: *The Perception of the Visual World.* Boston, Houghton, 1950; WYBURN, G. M., PICKFORD, R. W., HIRST, R. J.: *Human Senses and Perception*, U. of Toronto, 1964; HAMLYN, D. W.: *Sensation and Perception.* London, Routledge & Kegan Paul, 1961.

and modified by emotions in accordance with the welfare response brought about by inner determined forces resulting from heredity and adapted through experience.

Man perceives not only through visual signals but also through certain modulations of air vibrations. Our range of hearing is about from sixteen to sixteen thousand per second; for the most part, from one hundred to ten thousand. Thus, the high frequency signals that move a bat do not bestir us.

We perceive a sound, but we do not see it as such, nor are the air vibrations (which condition the sound) visible. Each sense, in short, responds to a different set of signals, and what we perceive is in and through a given sense and thus is limited to and in the sensory field in which the signal belongs.

We perceive an odor or we taste. Therein the stimulation of the sensory receptors (in our olfactory membranes or in our taste buds of the tongue) may be on the order of no more than one or two quanta of energy.

Signals of another order have to do with the tactile sense, protopathic and epicritic; with warm and cold perception; still another with pain; and so on, covering the gamut of the senses, not all of which are known.

Among the unknown or lesser known, the unrecognized or the insufficiently recognized signals of man are those which follow ingestion of food. These signals, in my observation, mark each step of the swallowing process and of the passage of food down the esophagus. These signals differ among themselves according to the chemical character of the food, its solid or fluid state, the size of the bolus and to some extent to the size of the particles which make up the bolus. We are largely indifferent to these details in signals, except that we integrate them when we say that we have eaten well or ill, feel comfortable or satisfied or the reverse. Close inspection of these signals after meals will reveal their vagueness, complexity and diversity.

Among the most important and most neglected of perceptive signals are those from the muscle sense, which participate in every effort, every emotion. These signals are triggered when the delicate nerve end organs in the muscle spindles are stretched upon muscular contraction. Attention to these signals is worth-

while, if cultivated, for they can tell us grossly how much energy
we are spending and where in each and every one of our efforts,
i.e., in our neuromuscular effort patterns.

Philosophers have argued among themselves in vain over the
questions: What is real? What is given to us by our senses? We
have seen above that these questions are not properly expressed.
Indeed, half the battle of science is won when the point is
reached where a question is expressed properly.

To perceive, we have seen, is to go out toward the stimulus, so
to speak, and to point out, employing another sense than the one
in which the signal appears. Speaking less figuratively, *perception
includes a highly vectorial neuromuscular response-pattern.* Perception is always an effort under the (often distorting) influence
of emotions according with our individual and collective welfare
responses.

Evaluation

To adapt and thrive in any set of external conditions, every
organism is obliged to evaluate them with respect to its own
welfare. Even the amoebae, exemplifying the primitive reactions
of unicellular organisms, must, so to speak, *evaluate* a fluid for
pinocytosis. I do not mean to read into the primitive drinking
response anything more than zoologists find objectively. The
reader may prefer to say that the amoeba acts as if the fluid were
evaluated. This is clear enough for our present discussion. I
repeat that we do not know and can not inquire whether unicellular organisms have primitive sensations, feelings or consciousness. We do not know this even about our own cells. However, it can prove useful if we realize that, if cells really are
devoid of primitive forms of consciousness, nevertheless they act
as if they were not altogether devoid. At some distant day of
the future some new way of testing for consciousness may be
discovered.

We can turn to man, however, for present-day information
about many of his conscious responses. For reliability, however,
human beings must be trained in observation and report. This
is educational routine in my clinic with many patients and
healthy subjects. They become highly skilled in distinguishing

signals from the meanings they convey. They become our "graduate students," and in my teaching experience in and out of university classes, often are comparable in this skill with those in university graduate departments.

Anyone can afford himself a quick experience of what I mean by evaluation if he will cross a city street crowded with automobile traffic. He sees a car approaching him as he crosses and for safety tends to estimate its speed relative to his own. He may hasten his steps to precede the oncoming car or may slow them in order to wait for its passage. If the road is slippery, he may take this into account, affecting his reactions one way or the other. Perhaps the car approaches with such speed as to frighten him. Then, in my belief, his esophagus tightens, thus carrying the message of fear.

In a later chapter the responses of the viscera in emotion will be discussed. Here let it suffice to say that, *in man, emotion is always a visceral, but always also a neuromuscular response.* The same words will apply to the function of evaluation in the welfare response; for, in most regards, the function of emotion is to accomplish evaluation in welfare.

When the cat in Cannon's laboratory was confronted with a dog, the cat showed arching of the back, retraction of the nicitating membrane, pilomotor response, scratching, spitting and movement toward or away from the dog. We can regard this as emotion or as evaluation of the hostile animal. Participation of the viscera was obvious: The alimentary tract became tense, and digestive processes ceased.

The same sort of occurrence is paralleled in man during anxious fright or panic. Sensations from the visceral and from the skeletal muscles, I find, make up the internal or subjective picture, as reported by our expert observers. The esophagus and other internal organs "evaluate" the situation; sensations from the viscera signal that the situation is dangerous.

Psychologists would do well to study the esophagus in action.[5]

---

[5] JACOBSON, E.: The physiology of globus hystericus. *JAMA*, 83:911-913, Sept. 20, 1924; Voluntary relaxation of the esophagus. *Amer. J. Physiol*, 72:387-394, May, 1925; Spastic esophagus and mucous colitis. *Trans. Sec. Gastroent. Proctol. A.M.A.*, 1926.

Darwin pointed out that when an animal frowns, it is a sign of meeting difficulty. They will find evidence, according to my experience, that the esophagus contracts likewise. Often during my personal work in mathematics, such as elliptic integrals, I have found myself in difficulty over some detail and have stopped working for a while. Upon asking myself why I stopped in place of keeping on, I have generally discerned that sensations from my esophagus apparently have inhibited my mathematical efforts.[6]

In emotion, then, as in evaluation, the esophagus plays a significant role. *What accounts for our conduct is not the situation as such, but the internal signals purporting to report the conditions to be met.*

It is common fallacy to say that this or that situation or condition "makes me nervous" or "makes me emotional." Meanings and significances do not cause phenomena occurring in accordance with Newton's first law any more than the messages conveyed over telegraph or telephone wires cause electrical or other changes. Obviously, what causes changes are not the meanings but the electrical impulses which signal the message.

Perhaps I can clarify by recalling a homely example—the automobile driver who continues to blow his horn on any pretext. What causes this? Popularly, we should reply, he blows his horn too often because he is in a hurry. However, in my experience, a differentially relaxed driver (I have known many) does not blow his horn so excessively, whether he is in a hurry or not. Accordingly, I should answer the question by saying that the drivers who make a practice of excessive horn blowing do so because their neuromusculature is excessively tense. Their tensions are triggered so that they respond irritably by blowing their horn to traffic conditions through which less irritable drivers would pass quietly.

Reflection

When situations and stimuli confront us lastingly we are led to reflect in the course of our welfare-effort response. From

---

[6] *Loc. cit.*

this point of view, reflection can be considered as prolonged evaluation, leading commonly to eventual decision or conclusion in action.

If the lasting situations and stimuli are menacing, many of us respond with anxiety. This is a form of welfare response familiarly seen among medical patients. I have reported on this previously from the clinic and laboratory, and further reports are in the offing.[7]

Tension states are identifiable in anxiety, whether neurotic or merely habitual. Evidence shows that with skeletal neuromuscular relaxation and habitual selective relaxation of anxiety-tension patterns, the emotion comes more or less under control. It is important, both for scientific and for practical reasons that suggestion and autosuggestion as well as forms of hypnosis be excluded.[8] In my experience, the anxious patient, whether hypochondriac or otherwise, becomes a dependent when the physician or psychologist relies on suggestive procedures. In contrast, the patient trained to observe his tension patterns and to relax them because it is he performing them and thus, he has the opportunity of not doing *becomes increasingly independent*, not only of his anxiety patterns, but also of the psychologist.

Thus, in the teaching of physiological operational techniques, we do not try to instill confidence, and we do not spend time in reassurance. The reader will understand that in this teaching field confidence plays no greater role than in teaching swimming or tennis or piano or flying a plane. In swimming the individual is prevented from sinking, not by his confidence but by his strokes. In flying the plane goes through the air in response to controls, not in response to the confidence of the operator. Accordingly, in relaxing the tensions of anxiety patterns, the therapeutic result does not depend chiefly on confidence. In some cases I have even seen anxiety patterns evidently diminish although confidence trailed far behind.

---

[7] *Anxiety and Tension Control.* Lippincott, 1964. *Modern Treatment of the Tension-Stress Complicating Every Illness* (to appear in 1967).

[8] JACOBSON, E.: Les principes soulignant les méthodes de la relaxation scientifique. *Rev. Med. Psychosom.*, 3(4):49-56, 1961.

Anxious reflection, then, is a familiar example of prolonged welfare response. I have summarized the influence of cultivating habitual differential relaxation in order to clarify the basic role of neuromuscular patterns which accompany the imagery. All our evidence indicates that these neuromuscular patterns are a necessary ingredient in anxiety, for when during whatsoever intervals they are present no longer, the total web of anxiety emotion likewise is absent.

Reflection, then, can be studied as prolonged evaluation. Present are not only visceral signal patterns but also neuromuscular patterns with the goal of solving the difficulty, finding a way toward welfare.

How is logical reflection carried out by man? I investigated this at Cornell during the 1910-11 college year, but have not heretofore published the conclusions. The procedure, I found, is not altogether different from a simple act such as arising to open a window. In this act I visualize the window being opened before I arise or while I arise from my chair. This visualization persists as I walk across the room toward the window. With the visualization, my recti eye muscles and others, often including those of the neck, contract as if to look toward the window. The visual image and eye muscle tension signals may wane as I proceed. Indeed, they may take the form of becoming less than observable, which I call subvisualization, accompanied by slight ocular muscle tension patterns measurable in action potentials (provided electrodes are placed under the eyes). Finally I reach the window, whereupon my sight, accompanied by tactile and pressure sensation, let me know that I am closing it, achieving my goal.

In reflection, I find the goal is visualized in some form, however varying and however symbolic to me of the solution I seek. Otherwise, prolonged reflection proceeds with facilitation and inhibitions to be sure, but on the whole in general terms as I have indicated in the goal of window closing.[9]

---

[9] In these observations, I have carried further the early observations of the psychologists of the Wuerzberger school, who left many problems with names but otherwise in murky darkness. I believe that these brilliant workers would have accomplished more if training in autosensory observations had been further advanced in their time.

Tension

We come to the fourth category in outlining the welfare response of man, namely, neuromuscular action, overt or miniscule.

Evaluation, including its prolonged form, reflection, culminates in action, which is overt neuromuscular response.

It would be fallacious to believe that the welfare response consists of four steps successively occurring one after another, namely, perception, evaluation, reflection and tension or overt decisive action. Much can be said about this.

I have found upon autosensory studies and have confirmed with action-potential measurements that perception never (in my studies) is exclusively a sensory response. Considerations to this effect have been set forth above. Our investigations disclose that the ocular muscles act during visualization of imagination, recall and emotion in much the same fashion (but with less action-potential voltage as a rule) as when the same person sees an object with open eyelids. When a sound is perceived, the eyes move as if in the direction of the imagined sound. Analogous ocular tensions appear when an odor is perceived. (What has been said applies to persons born with sight. I presume that in the congenital blind, kinesthetic and tactile sensations become the signals adducent in perception, but this remains to be investigated.)

For clarification, let us return to the simple example of the person who crosses the street in traffic dangerously congested. When he sees the oncoming car about to cross his own path, his eye muscles tense accordingly. However if there is real danger, he sees the car at the very first instant of clear perception as a dangerous vehicle and as part of that very perception he tenses the muscles of his legs, trunk and perhaps other parts in preliminary withdrawal. Again, the father perceives his favorite little daughter, not first as a youthful human being and later as his love, towards whom he moves and otherwise tenses in affection, but instead he perceives and regards her as his lovely possession from the very first instant of his full perception. Trained observers confirm this. Many psychologists have written in the same report.

Likewise, in evaluation, skeletal neuromuscular tensions as outlined above play an indispensible role. This subject has been dis-

Brain-Neuromuscular Welfare Response In Man

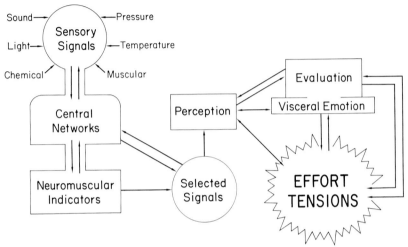

FIGURE 1. Schematic of the welfare response in man. As in an analog computer, but on a much more complicated scale, there is *programming* with acceptance of certain "information" and rejection of other.[1] Perception of environment occurs through information processing in the nervous system. Signals proceeding from and representing internal and environmental conditions to the organism apparently are "scanned" and certain ones are "selected" for evaluation and motor response. However, even in this first stage, skeletal neuromuscular response evidently plays a role (see text). The selection (subjectively studied) consists of neuromuscular processes which "point to" or "designate" certain of the signals. (This is popularly known as *attention* [see text].) Visceral muscle reacts as part of the evaluation function. Appropriate motor response occurs to what the total organism thus finds significant. Recurrent arrows serve to indicate the interinvolvement of perceptual, evaluational and effort responses. ([1]Learning tension control is basically changing the programming within the system to produce desired end-results.)

cussed in the references cited and also will be discussed in later chapters herein.

The four phases of conscious response—perception, evaluation, reflection and neuromuscular action—have been extensively studied in the past by many investigators, but from unintegrated points of view, thus different from the present. References to their investigations would be a desirable task but of encyclopedic

Perception-Evaluation-Tension

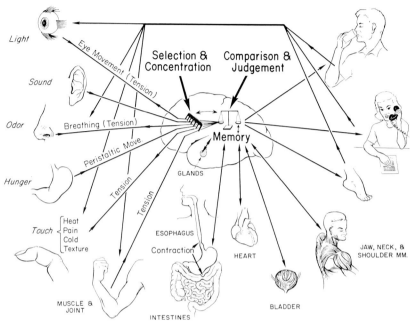

FIGURE 2. The universal PET welfare reaction. Suggested complexity of the incessant PET adaptive response in man and lower animals. Abnormalities in this response distinguish the various disorders of neuropsychiatry. Thus in anxiety tension there is dysevaluation (as also in depressed states).

complexity. Therefore I have preferred to be clear in outline, rather than confusing with detailed examples and illustrations; to picture the forest rather than to become lost among the trees. The cost has been a certain lack of precision for which, I hope, the gain in exposition can compensate (see Figs. 1 and 2).

However, precision can stem from future investigations in other laboratories and clinics as well as my own. The patterns of residual neuromuscular tension now discernible only to subjects long trained in autosensory observation and meaning statement need to be studied by more precise methods than are presently available to science. I look forward perhaps a decade or two, when computers commonly named "Adeline" and "Nadeline" may be applied to oscilloscope patterns on the oscilloscope. We have been recording such patterns extensively for years in the present investigations but must wait for the attainment of adequate computer systems. Why say anything about residual patterns till then? Because their occurrence is definitely observable upon careful autosensory observation and it is therefore a step forward to emphasize their importance in emotion. Science, like Rome, is not built in a day.

Integration of the Welfare Response

What I have discussed above might well have been entitled "The Integrative Welfare Response of the Neuromuscular System." In reading Sherrington's prophetic book, I was always impressed with how little we knew about integration when it was written. I continue to be so impressed even today.

However, we can say of integration in the nervous system, particularly in the brain, that through networks or other means of as yet unknown character and complexity, the welfare response commonly proceeds in orderly fashion and leads to a desirable end.

This is not always true. In anxiety neurosis the welfare response generally is too intense in the tensions (measured in microvolts) and is too long drawn out. One of the aims of therapy is to lessen and shorten these responses.

We are reminded of another type of welfare response—inflammation. This response of body fluids and cells, like anxiety and various other forms of emotional response, can be and often is carried too far. Modern therapy against excessive inflammation often consists of administration of ACTH or of corticosteroids. Thereby repair is slowed, sometimes to advantage. Integration here is not exclusively a nervous function, but in part is endocrine. There is suggestive evidence that in emotion, likewise, integration rests partly on the endocrine system.

We have seen that to understand emotion, we need to take into account the welfare response. In the following chapter, as we review the investigations of emotional behavior in animals, it may become apparent that neglect of this aspect may account for the scattered nature of this field of knowledge up to date and the lack of a unifying point of view.

Chapter III

EMOTIONAL BEHAVIOR

Human Self-observation Indispensible

ACCORDING to most psychologists, including those of the diverse schools of W. Wundt, W. James, E. B. Titchener and S. Freud, anxiety and other emotions are "in the first place something felt" or experienced. To this I would add that to know an emotion requires personal experience just as to know the character of vision or of audition requires seeing form or color or hearing sounds. To one born blind, for example, the color green is indescribable.

If the psychologists mentioned are correct, we cannot fully delineate or describe the nature of the emotions when we confine ourselves exclusively to emotional behavior. Something essential will be missing—something which introspection (autosensory observation) alone can furnish. Unfortunately, however, autosensory observation is currently neglected in most university departments of psychology. In a sense we can make ourselves blind to the nature of emotions if we continue this basic neglect.

This is not to say that emotional behavior should be neglected. For the most part this is studied in laboratory animals. However, even the most ingenious application of Pavlovian or other laboratory method will not lead to the cat or other animal telling us clearly about his experience. In particular investigations, we do not learn whether the animal really experiences an emotion or not, as in studies of so-called sham rages. Furthermore, many important emotions, such as shame, embarrassment, grief, love, hate and guilt, largely elude laboratory investigation based on animal behavior.

These considerations appear essential in order to effect a balanced understanding of the emotions, *which is attainable scien-*

tifically by subjective no less than by behavioristic methods. It should be recognized that both approaches are indispensible. Largely limited to the latter is the otherwise thorough review of emotional behavior under the authorship of J. V. Brady, from which I shall draw in the present chapter, but the reader is urged to refer to it directly.[1] I shall draw also from E. Gellhorn's *Physiological Foundations of Neurology and Psychiatry.*[2]

Emotion Defined

Brady's account is hampered also, he states, since, "in the rather obvious absence of any completely satisfactory theoretical or experimental formulation of emotional behavior, the task of defining and delimiting the psychological subject matter for such a neurophysiological survey can be seen to present many difficulties."[3] To supply this want, the definition of emotion submitted in Chapter VI, p. 87, will serve in the present text.[4]

Data from laboratory studies on emotion relate to vegetative nervous responses, including salivation and its measurement, psychogalvanic reflex action, sweating, blood pressure and volume, heart rate and cardiogram, respiration, temperature, pupillary changes, pilomotor phenomena, dermatographia, chemical composition of the blood, saliva and urine. In our laboratory and clinic, many quantitative studies have been made on muscular contraction (effort-tension) and relaxation, peripheral nerve activity and quiet, basal metabolism, arterial hyptertension, eye blink and eye movements. Presently, the relation of central neural organization in human emotional behavior is being studied extensively.

In animals, the methods employed in emotions research derive from ablation of nervous structures, electrical or chemical stimulation thereof, electrical recording therefrom, lately with implanted electrodes and clinical, mostly postsurgical observations.

---

[1] BRADY, J. V.: *Emotional behavior.* In Field, J., *et al.* (Eds.): *Handbook of Physiology,* Vol. III. Washington, D. C., Amer. Physiol. Soc., 1960, pp. 1529-1552.

[2] U. of Minn., 1953.

[3] *Loc. cit.,* p. 1530.

[4] Definitions are of four types: (a) they set forth essential character, or (b) they only describe; or (c) they delimit; or (d) they only illustrate or give examples.

The Sympathetic Discharge in Emotion

In 1925, Cannon and Britton found that the denervated hearts of laboratory animals showed increased rates (such as 252 per minute) which fell (e.g., to 151) if the adrenal glands were removed. They inferred that in the pseudoaffective state of emotional excitement, there occurs a great increase of medullary adrenal secretion."[5] Cannon and his associates made many studies of apparent states of anxiety, fear and anger in laboratory animals which disclosed cardiovascular and gastrointestinal phenomena, among them many of the same general type as I have described in human beings[6] and shall outline in Chapter VIII. They found what in the present text are termed *tension states* and *tension disorders*. Evidently pertinent to these states and disorders in man are methods of relaxation, which will be described herein.

Parasympathetic Discharge in Emotion

In carefully controlled studies, E. Gellhorn *et al.* showed that the visceral discharge during emotion is not limited to the sympatheticoadrenal system but concerns the vagoinsulin system as well. Their results pointed to activation of the internal secretion of the pancreas via the vagus, lowering the blood sugar (unless counterbalanced by sympathetic discharge).[7] Cannon emphasized the importance of increased blood sugar for fight and flight and other emotional emergencies. Gellhorn points out that hyperglycemic reaction combined with increased insulin secretion provides optimal conditions. Contraction of the bladder, defecation and erection of the penis are further signs of parasympathetic discharge.[8]

[5] CANNON, W. B., and BRITTON, S. W.: Studies on the conditions of activity in endocrine glands. XV. Pseudoaffective medulliadrenal secretion. *Amer. J. Physiol.,* 72:283-294, 1925.

[6] JACOBSON, EDMUND: *Progressive Relaxation.* U. of Chicago, rev. ed., 1938.

[7] GELLHORN, E., CORTELL, R., and FELDMAN, J.: The effect of emotion, sham rage and hypothalamic stimulation on the vago-insulin system. *Amer. J. Physiol., 133:* 532-541, 1941.

[8] HUNT, W. A., LANDIS, C., and JACOBSEN, C. F.: Studies of the startle pattern. V. Apes and monkeys. *J. Psychol.,* 3:339-343, 1937.

Autonomic Discharges in Human Anxiety and Other Emotion

Todd and Rowlands found that anxiety and tenseness are marked by a loss of tone and a decrease in the amplitude of contractions of the stomach and intestinal musculature with prolonged emptying time.[9] In anxiety and other types of human emotion, signs of sympathetic overactivity include increased blood pressure and heart rate as well as viscous salivary secretion and palmar sweating.[10]

Parasympathetic signs of human overemotionality presumably can include increased frequency of urination with or without defecation,[11] and even weeping.[12] Portis claimed that low blood sugar is characteristic in states of human anxiety and stress[13] and recommended anticholinergic treatment (atropine). In nine instances I have failed to confirm this finding.[14] Further studies are needed.

Evidently, both branches of the autonomic nervous system may participate in emotion, but with individual differences in the vascular[15] as well as in the alimentary system.[16]

Even in the same person, according to Wolf *et al.,* similar vascular, secretory and motor responses may characterize different emotional states such as pleasure and anxiety. It is suggested that fear is marked predominantly by sympathetic, anxiety and hostility

---

[9] TODD, T. W., and ROWLANDS, M. E.: Studies in alimentary canal of man; emotional interference in gastric behavior patterns. *J. Comp. Psychol., 10:*167-188, 1930.

[10] DARROW, C. W.: The galvanic skin reflex (sweating) and blood pressure as preparatory and facilitative functions., *Psychol. Bull., 33:*73-94, 1936.

[11] ALVAREZ, W. C.: Ways in which emotion can affect the digestive tract. *JAMA, 92:*1231-1237, 1929; DUMAS, G.: Le choc emotionel. *J. Psychol. Norm. Path., 25:* 130-164, 1928; JANET, J.: *Les Troubles Psychopathiques de la Miction. Paris,* Lefrancois, 1890.

[12] LUND, F. H.: Why do we weep? *J. Soc. Psychol., 1:*136-151, 1930.

[13] PORTIS, S. A.: Life situations, emotions and hyperinsulinism. *JAMA, 142:*1281-1286, 1950

[14] Unpublished studies.

[15] WEBER, E.: *Der Einfluss psychischer Vorgänge auf den Körper, insbesondere auf die Blutverteilung.* Berlin, Springer, 1910; RICHTER, D.: Somatic aspects of mental health and disease. *Brit. Med. Bull., 6:*44-48, 1949.

[16] WOLF, S., and WOLFF, H. G.: *Human Gastric Function.* New York, Oxford U. P., 2nd ed., 1947; WOLFF, H. G.: Life situations, emotions and the large bowel. *Trans. Ass. Amer. Physicians, 62:*192-195, 1949.

by parasympathetic discharges.[17] After vagotomy, anxiety failed to produce (parasympathetic) effects on the stomach. Anxiety and resentment were marked by parasympathetic reactions also in the vagina (hyperemia and increased discharge) and in the bladder (increased tone and vascularity), accounting for diminished capacity. After such functional overactivity had persisted, edema and hemorrhage from mucous membranes seemed to follow in the stomach and intestines.

The words *anger, shame, anxiety* should not mislead us to believe that each emotion has a constant physiological basis, any more than the word *home* should mislead us to assume that all dwellings have a common architecture. In anxiety states recounted from nineteen clinical investigations, no two were really alike.[18] Accordingly, also, Hickam *et al.* found varying cardiovascular effects in different individuals. The cardiac output, oxygen consumption and heart rate were increased in most, while the peripheral resistance was lowered. This was interpreted as a sympatheticoadrenalin discharge. Another group showed signs of parasympathetic activation, namely, diminished heart rate, lowered blood pressure and decreased resistance. The liberation of noradrenalin was suggested in a small group, with increased blood pressure and peripheral resistance.[19]

Brain Localization in Emotion

In 1929, P. Bard studied sham rage in forty-six decorticate cats. He found that this occurs regularly after ablation of the hemispheres, corpora striata and the cranial half of the diencephalon, but invariably failed to develop when the brain stem was tran-

---

[17] Opinions differ. Ax studied human fear and anger, recording skin conductance, muscle potentials, pulse, respiration, face and hand temperature and other variables. He interpreted his results as contrary to the proposal that "anger is a strong reaction of both the sympathetic and parasympathetic branches of the autonomic nervous system, whereas fear is but a sympathetic reaction." Ax, A. F.: The physiological differentiation between fear and anger in humans. *Psychosom. Med.*, 15(5):442, Sept.-Oct., 1953; ARNOLD, M.: An excitatory theory of emotion. In REYMERT, M. L. (Ed.): *Feelings and Emotions.* New York, McGraw, 1950, Chapter 2.

[18] *Loc. cit.*

[19] HICKAM, J. B., CARGILL, W. H. and GOLDEN, A.: Cardiovascular reactions to emotional stimuli. *J. Clin. Invest.*, 27:290-298, 1948.

sected at the caudal extremity of the diencephalon or through the cranial portion of the mesencephalon. The central mechanisms of sham rage, he concluded, lie within an area comprising the caudal half of the hypothalamus and the most ventral and most caudal fractions of the corresponding segment of the thalamus.[20]

Knowledge of the functions of the thalamus or of the hypothalamus were thus advanced by Cannon and by Bard, but also by other investigators, including Penfield and Ranson.[21]

Papez Theory of Localization

In 1937, Papez was led to propose "a mechanism of emotion." This related to reciprocal connections between the anterior thalamic nuclei, the hypothalamus and the gyrus cinguli and the hippocampus, mediating, by means of the cortical circuit, the function of emotion.[22] In a sense, the theory of Papez is an outgrowth and development of that of Cannon. It led to the following comment by Brady: "A few months later (in 1937), Papez's speculative paper on 'A Proposed Mechanism of Emotion' appeared with its emphasis upon primarily paleocortical, juxtallocortical and related subcortical structures; and in the following two dec-

---

[20] BARD, P.: The central representation of the sympathetic system. Arch. Neurol. and Psychiat. (Chicago), 22(2):230-246, Aug., 1929.

[21] PENFIELD, W.: Influence of the diencephalon and hypophysis upon general autonomic function. Bull. N.Y. Acad. Med., 9:613-637, 1933; Canad. Med. Ass. J., 30:589-598, June, 1934; RANSON, S. W.: The hypothalamus: Its significance for visceral innervation and emotional expression. Trans. Coll. Physicians Phila., 2: 222-242, 1934.

[22] PAPEZ, J. W.: A proposed mechanism of emotion. Arch. Neurol. and Psychiat. (Chicago), 38:(4)725-743, Oct., 1937. "Cogent argument," he states, "can be drawn in support of the view that the gyrus cinguli is the seat of dynamic vigilance by which evironmental experiences are endowed with an emotional consciousness."

Dandy removed the various lobes of the hemispheres and ligated the left anterior cerebral artery and noted the effect on consciousness. He localized the seat of consciousness along the mesial aspect of the left hemisphere and near the corpus callosum (DANDY, W. E.: Seat of consciousness. In LEWIS, D.: Practice of Surgery. Hagerstown, W. F. Prior Co., 1931, 12:37. Bailey reports that consciousness, heavily dependent upon the cerebral cortex, both in animals and in man, is similarly dependent upon "a small destruction in the neighborhood of the aqueduct of Sylvius." (BAILEY, PERCIVAL: Modern attitudes toward the relationship of the brain to behavior. Arch. Gen. Psychiat. (Chicago), 2(4):366, April, 1960).

ades, numerous anatomical, neurophysiological and behavioral studies have testified to the truly remarkable perspicacity of these early efforts."[23]

Hypothalamus in Emotion

Most important among contributions on the role of the hypothalamus in emotional behavior have been those of W. R. Hess.[24] His technique of stimulating selected subcortical structures with implanted electrodes has brought dramatic results, as when the animal is led to assume a typical defense posture, extends its claws and lashes its tail, hisses, spits, growls, retracts its ears, with wide open pupils and eyes and hair erect on back and tail. Hess calls this the "affective defense reaction." At this stage of general excitement a slight move on the part of an observer arouses a brisk and well-directed assault. Positive results of this sort were obtained not only upon stimulation in the hypothalamus but also in the preoptic and ventral septal region and in the central (periaqueductal) gray matter of the midbrain. Ranson and Magoun were led by their findings to conclude that "the hypothalamus is concerned primarily with the control of visceral functions."[25] Ingram writes: "It has been pointed out by Ranson and others that the responses to direct stimulation of the hypothalamus are of a nature which if observed in normal waking cats would be associated with anger, fear, or some such emotion. . . . The hypothalamus may be concerned with integration of the sympathetic phases of response to stimuli tending to produce behavior of an emotional type."[26]

---

[23] BRADY, op. cit., p. 1532.

[24] HESS, W. R., and AKERT, K.: Experimental data on role of hypothalamus in mechanism of emotional behavior. Arch. Neurol. and Psychiat. (Chicago) 73(2): 127-129, Feb., 1955. Stimulation of the posterior part of the hypothalamus is marked by increased motor excitability culminating in rage (sympathetic discharge), while stimulation of the anterior part effects diminished muscle tone and motor excitability (parasympathetic discharge) (Vegetative Funktionen und Zwischenhirn. Basel, Schwabe, 1947).

[25] RANSON, S. W., and MAGOUN, H. W.: The hypothalamus, Ergebn. Physiol., 41: 56, 1939.

[26] INGRAM, W. R.: Hypothalamus; A review of the experimental data. Psychosom. Med. 1:77, Jan., 1939.

Gellhorn rejects Masserman's conclusion that the hypophysis is "a motor center only," since he has shown that stimulation of this center "leads to definite cortical changes."[27] Reviewing the studies of Hess, he adds: "These observations strongly suggest that the whole complex of emotion may be elicited by electrical stimulation of the hypothalamus."[28]

Studies on the role of hypothalamic region in emotion have become too numerous to recount here. A fuller account is rendered in E. Gellhorn's monumental volume, *Physiological Foundations of Neurology and Psychiatry*. For various other points of view (on the part of reviewers as well as of investigators), the reader is referred to the recent reviews of Brady[29] and of A. Simon[30], but also to the earlier reviews of Rapaport and of Dunbar.[31]

The Neocortex in Emotion

The studies of Klüver and Bucy are well known. Following bilateral temporal lobectomy in the rhesus monkey, the animals showed psychic blindness. Instead of using their eyes, they generally examined all objects by mouth. "We find either profound changes in emotional behavior or complete absence of all emotional reactions in the sense that the motor and vocal reactions

---

[27] GELLHORN, E.: *Physiological Foundations of Neurology and Psychiatry.* Minn., U. of Minn., 1953, p. 341; MURPHY, J. P., and GELLHORN, E.: Influence of hypothalamic stimulation on cortically induced movements and action potentials of the cortex. *J. Neurophysiol.,* 8:341-364, 1945.

[28] *Ibid.,* p. 341.

[29] BRADY, *loc. cit.*

[30] SIMON, A.: *The Physiology of Emotions,* Springfield, Thomas, 1961.

[31] DUNBAR, F.: *Emotions and Bodily Changes.* New York, Columbia, 1954; RAPAPORT, D.: *Emotions and Memory* New York, Int. Univs., 1950. In his review, Hypothalamic functions in psychosomatic interrelations, *Psychosom. Med.,* 1:25-26, Jan., 1939, R. R. Grinker writes: "Not only does the hypothalamus integrate all of visceral and autonomic activity but it functions as a balancing mechanism between parasympathetic and orthosympathetic divisions. The parasympathetic system is associated with anabolism, lessening the efficiency of the sensorimotor system and operating in the interest of individual organs. It furnishes the brake upon activities, conserves resources and reserves and builds up tensions. The orthosympathetic system lies exterior to the visceral organs and enhances the functions of the sensory motor apparatus, increasing the functional output. It is concerned with catabolic activity in massively discharging internal systems."

generally associated with anger and fear are not exhibited. This change in affectivity is especially remarkable in view of the fact that care has been taken to use only 'wild' aggressive monkeys in this work."[32] Somewhat similar findings were reported by Fulton *et al.*, following bilateral ablation of the frontotemporal portion of the juxtallocortex in monkeys.[33]

Limbic System

Sham rage reactions were observed by Spiegel *et al.* following lesions in the more rostral portions of the limbic system in both cats and dogs—lesions confined to the olfactory tubercle and septal region or from involvement of the anterior amygdaloid nuclei, parts of the hippocampus and the fornix. Somewhat similar reactions had been observed by Fulton and Ingraham following bilateral prechiasmal lesions at the base of the brain.

Following analysis of the results of psychosurgery, Spiegel *et al.* concluded "that it is not possible to refer emotional reactions to a single circumscribed nucleus within the diencephalon or its connections with the frontal lobes, but that there exists a multiple representation of this function. Following the elimination of one or two of these circuits others are able to compensate for the loss."[34] However, ablations in animals and lesions in psychiatric patients involving chiefly the dorsomedial nuclei of the thalamus, seemed to reduce anxiety, tension, agitation and aggressive or assaultive behavior.

Conditioned anxiety in monkeys was produced by Delgado through electrical stimulation of cerebral structures in the tegmentum, central gray substance around the aqueduct, the pos-

---

[32] KLÜVER, H., and BUCY, P.: Preliminary analysis of functions of the temporal lobes in monkeys. *Arch. Neurol. and Psychiat. (Chicago)*, Dec., 1939, pp. 42, 979 and 986.

[33] FULTON, J. F., PRIBRAM, K. H., STEVENSON, J. A., and WALL, P. D.: Interrelations between orbital gyrus, insula, temporal tip and anterior cingulate. *Trans. Amer. Neurol. Ass.*, 74:175, 1949.

[34] SPIEGEL, E. A., WYCIS, H. T., FREED, H., and ARCHINIK, C.: The central mechanism of the emotions (experiences with circumscribed thalamic lesions). *Amer. J. Psychiat.* 108:426, 1951; FULTON, J. F., and INGRAHAM, F. D. Emotional disturbances following experimental lesions of the brain (pre-chiarmal). *J. Physiol.*, 67:27, 1929.

teroventral nucleus of the thalamus and the crus formicis of the hippocampus. Anxiety was interpreted upon attempts to escape, biting and restlessness.[35] Unanesthetized cats showed reactions of bewilderment, anxiety and sometimes fear, anger and fury, along with contralateral searching movements upon stimulation of the amygdaloid nucleus (in the phylogenetically younger basolateral division).[36] As related by Olds and Milner in their famous studies: "There are numerous places in the lower centers of the (rat) brain where electrical stimulation is rewarding in the sense that the experimental animal (rat) will stimulate itself in these places frequently and regularly for long periods of time if permitted to do so. It is possible to obtain these results from as far back as the tegmentum and as far forward as the septal area; from as far down as the subthalamus and as far up as the cingulate gyrus of the cortex. . . . There are also sites in the lower centers where the effect is just the opposite: animals do everything possible to avoid stimulation."[37]

Quite recently, F. Isamat electrically stimulated points in the medial wall of the cerebral cortex in twelve cats, recording galvanic skin responses in all four feet. Positive results were obtained most readily from the anterior limbic and the infralimbic areas of the cortex anterior to and under the rostrum of the corpus callosum.[38]

In addition to the foregoing studies, many others of recent decades bear upon emotional behavior. Much evidence has been gathered favoring the participation of neural components of the limbic lobe (see Figs. 3 and 4). A summary account is presented by P. D. MacLean, who begins as follows: "The limbic system is comprised of the great limbic lobe of Broca and its subcortical cell stations. The limbic lobe, including the infolded hippocam-

[35] DELGADO, J. M. R.: Cerebral structures involved in transmission and elaboration of noxious stimulation. *J. Neurophysiol.*, 18:265, May, 1955.

[36] KAADA, B. R., ANDERSEN, P., and JANSEN, JR., J.: Stimulation of the amygdaloid nuclear complex in unanesthetized cats. *Neurology*, 4:48-64, 1954.

[37] OLDS, J., and MILNER, P.: Positive reinforcement produced by electrical stimulation of septal area and other regions of rat brain. *J. Comp. Physiol. Psychol.*, 47:419-427, Dec., 1954.

[38] ISAMAT, F.: Galvanic skin responses from stimulation of limbic cortex. *J. Neurophysiol.*, *XXIV* (2):176-181, March, 1961.

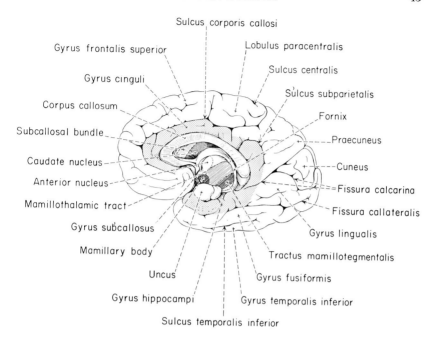

Sulcus corporis callosi
Gyrus frontalis superior
Lobulus paracentralis
Gyrus cinguli
Sulcus centralis
Corpus callosum
Sulcus subparietalis
Subcallosal bundle
Fornix
Caudate nucleus
Praecuneus
Anterior nucleus
Cuneus
Mamillothalamic tract
Fissura calcarina
Gyrus subcallosus
Fissura collateralis
Mamillary body
Gyrus lingualis
Uncus
Tractus mamillotegmentalis
Gyrus hippocampi
Gyrus fusiformis
Sulcus temporalis inferior
Gyrus temporalis inferior

Right Cerebral Hemisphere, viewed from the left, partly schematic.

FIGURE 3. Right cerebral hemisphere, viewed from the left, partly schematic. Limbic cortex is marked by stippling. (Adapted from Spalteholz *Anatomy*, drawing by R. E. Lange.)

pus, was so named by Broca because it completely surrounds the hilus of the hemisphere. Its subcortical cell stations include the amygdala, the septal nuclei, the hypothalamus, the anterior thalamic nuclei, parts of the basal ganglia and perhaps also the epithalamus."[39]

In his review, Brady comments significantly: "No completely satisfactory integration of the limbic system with the necessarily broad range of central neural participants in emotional behavior has as yet emerged."[40]

[39] MacLean, P. D.: The limbic system ("visceral brain") and emotional behavior. *Arch. Neurol. (Chicago)*, 73:130, Feb., 1955; Some psychiatric implications of physiological studies of frontotemporal portion of limbic system (visceral brain). *Electroenceph. Clin. Neurophysiol.*, IV (4):407-418, Nov., 1952.

[40] Brady, *op. cit.*, p. 1541.

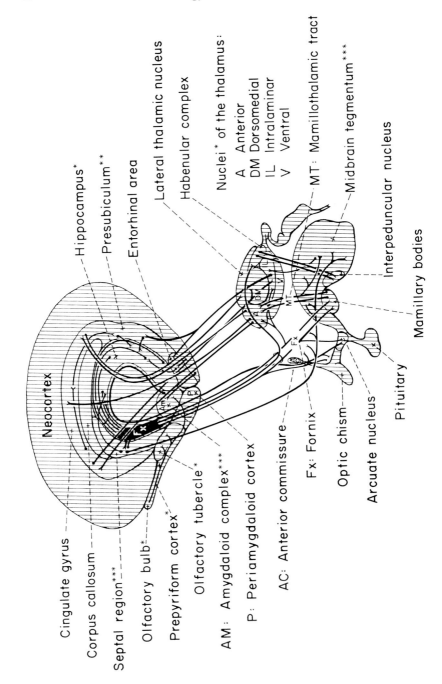

Neocortex

Cingulate gyrus

Corpus callosum

Septal region***

Olfactory bulb*

Prepyriform cortex

Olfactory tubercle*

AM: Amygdaloid complex***

P: Periamygdaloid cortex

AC: Anterior commissure

Fx: Fornix

Optic chism

Arcuate nucleus

Pituitary

Hippocampus*

Presubiculum**

Entorhinal area

Lateral thalamic nucleus

Habenular complex

Nuclei* of the thalamus:
A   Anterior
DM Dorsomedial
IL Intralaminar
V   Ventral

MT: Mamillothalamic tract

Midbrain tegmentum***

Interpeduncular nucleus

Mamillary bodies

We can pause, then, to scan the horizon for possibilities, especially MacLean's view of the importance of these forebrain structures for sensations from the mouth, the viscera, the sex organs, the body wall, the eye and the ear; or Pribram and Kruger's view of olfactory-gustatory, metabolic and socioemotional functions of limbic components. In general, investigators on neural elements in emotional behavior evidently have made great progress, often with elaboration of important theories, which as a rule they have clearly demarcated from their observations. To be sure, our understanding of this vastly complicated field is still in its infancy.

Frontal Lobes

Complexities multiply upon consideration of the interplay of neocortex and limbic lobe in emotional behavior. Modern study of frontal lobe function in emotional behavior was discussed and to a certain extent introduced by L. Bianchi.[41] Subsequently,

Psychosurgery

ablation procedures were introduced into psychosurgery in certain emotional disorders.[42] Recently, P. Bailey considers the

---

[41] BIANCHI, L.: *The Mechanism of the Brain and the Function of the Frontal Lobes* [Trans.] MacDonald, J. H. New York, Wood, 1922.

[42] MONIZ, E.: *Tentatives Operatoires dans le Traitment de Certaines Psychoses.* Paris, Masson, 1936.

←

FIGURE 4. Diagram of the limbic system and related or adjacent tracts. Some structures included in the paleocortex (the region of phylogenetic primacy) are marked by one star. Some other structures included in the juxtallocortical portions of the limbic system (that group intermediate in position between the phylogenetically old paleocortex and the phylogenetically young neocortex) are marked by two stars. Certain subcortical structures belonging to the limbic system are marked by three stars. (Adapted from BRADY, J. V.: Emotional behavior. In the *Handbook of Physiology, Neurophysiology III*. Washington, D. C., American Physiological Society, 1960. Chapter LXIII, p. 1537 [Fig. 1]. Drawing by R. E. Lange).

results disappointing and the surgery of dubious value.[43] On the other hand, C. Landis reports that psychosurgery, extirpating frontal lobe tissue or cutting of frontothalamic tracts, relieves the patient of intractable pain or intolerable anguish in psychosis or neurosis.[44] For further studies on neocortical participation in emotion, the reader is referred to Brady's review.[45]

Miscellaneous
Investigations on Anxiety

A miscellany of investigations on anxiety, some of considerable importance, will be mentioned in the following pages of this chapter. We turn to electroencephalographic studies.

EEG in Anxiety

Berger, and later Adrian, recognized that the level of awareness and the subject's anxiety influenced the suppression of alpha activity. K. H. Finley found fast activity in a wide range of psychiatric disorders involving anxiety and overactivity.[46] Various investigators, in short, report the presence of beta waves in anxiety states. Hill discussed this matter in 1950.[47]

A. C. Mundy-Castle presented data suggesting that beta activity may in part at least represent accelerated rhythms resultant on scansion of cortical projection and association areas. He believes that augmentation of theta rhythm may parallel increasing unpleasure.[48] As for psychiatric disorders involving anxiety and overactivity, he states (italics mine): "*In this connection an ob-*

[43] BAILEY, P.: The academic lecture. The great psychiatric revolution. *Amer. J. Psychiat.* *113*(5):387-406, Nov., 1956.

[44] LANDIS, CAREY: Remarks on psychological findings attendant on psychosurgery. In *The Biology of Mental Health and Disease*. New York, Hoeber, 1952 The interested reader is referred to METTLER, F. A. (Ed.): *Selective Partial Ablation of the Frontal Cortex*. New York, Hoeber, 1949.

[45] BRADY, *loc. cit.*, pp. 1542-1543.

[46] FINLEY, K. H.: On the occurence of rapid frequency potential changes in the human electroencephalogram. *Amer. J. Psychiat.*, *101*:194-200, 1944.

[47] HILL, D., and PARR, G. (Eds.): *Electroencephalography—A Symposium on its Various Aspects*. London, Macdonald, 1950, Chapter XI.

[48] MUNDY-CASTLE, A. C.: Theta and beta rhythm in the electroencephalograms of normal adults. *Electroenceph. Clin. Neurophysiol.*, 3(4):486, Nov., 1951. In his "young adult group," he reports mean frequency of beta activity at a little less than 18 cps and mean amplitude 8.74 microvolts.

vious difficulty is that of muscle tension, a common feature in anxiety."

M. A. Kennard stated that "it is certain that the schizophrenics show marked anxiety tension." Bickford found that his "schizophrenic patients relax rather less well than other patients," which led him to question whether muscle action-potentials possibly contributed to the fast frequencies in Kennard's electroencephalograms. She "did not know the answer."[49]

On the other hand, recording from the regions of the thalamus and hypothalamus failed to yield characteristic curves in anxiety: "Significant differences between the records of the various groups of patients could not be found, the cases of anxiety neurosis probably representing records most nearly close to normal."[50]

In the publications mentioned above, we see that the beta frequencies reported by many of the observers in anxiety states have not always been distinguished from possible muscle action-potentials which have not been excluded from the electroencephalogram. A still more important difficulty in attempting to correlate beta or other fast frequencies with anxiety emotion is the present lack of means to determine whether the increased frequencies are attributable to anxiety emotion or to increased cortical or subcortical activity attendant upon a generally increased state of central nervous activity. Indeed, it is common experience among electroencephalographers that beta and other fast frequencies commonly occur also in the absence of anxiety emotion. In anxiety, as compared with relaxed sleep, the cortex exhibits what have been termed electrical *arousal effects,* but arousal effects commonly occur without accompaniment of anxiety.[51]

---

[49] KENNARD, M. A., RABINOVITCH, S., and FISTER, W.: The use of frequency analysis in the interpretation of the EEGs of patients with psychological disorders. *Electroenceph. Clin. Neurophysiol.,* 6(4):702, Nov., 1954.

[50] SPIEGEL, E. A., and WYCIS, H. T.: Thalamic and hypothalamic electrograms in psychoses. *Electroenceph. Clin. Neurophysiol.,* 6(4):702-703, Nov. 1954.

[51] Cf. CHOH-LUH, L., JASPER, H., and HENDERSON, L., JR.: The effect of arousal mechanisms on various forms of abnormality in the electroencephalogram. *Electroenceph. Clin. Neurophysiol.,* IV, 4:513, Nov., 1952. "Renewed interest in the effects of arousal, sleep and waking responses upon the electrical activity of the cortex," they write, "has come from the demonstration of an ascending reticular activating system of the brain-stem, which appears to mediate such effects."

J. B. Hickam *et al.* found that cardiovascular phenomena varied in anxiety states. In the majority, the cardiac output, oxygen consumption and heart rate were increased while the peripheral resistance was diminished. In others, the resistance was decreased, as were the heart rate (vagus) and the blood pressure. In a small proportion the peripheral resistance and the blood pressure were increased. Possibly the first group showed predominantly a sympatheticoadrenalin discharge, the second a parasympathetic innervation and the third the liberation of noradrenalin.[52]

Endocrine and Biochemical Studies

Grinker *et al.* have written a series of articles, the first of which was entitled, "A Theoretical and Experimental Approach to Problems of Anxiety."[53] In previous work they had utilized soldiers with war neuroses, civilians in panic or anxiety states and paratroopers in training.[54]

A second article by the Michael Reese team deals with an experimental study of twenty-one patients having "in common some degree of anxiety or anxiety proneness." They found the "9:00 A.M. plasma level of hydrocortisone on the 'base-day' about 60 percent greater in the anxious subjects than in either of the control groups."[55] They studied also some of the hydrocortisone

---

[52] HICKAM, J. B., CARGILL, W. H., and GOLDEN, A.: Cardiovascular reactions to emotional stimuli. Effect on the cardiac output, arteriovenous oxygen difference, arterial pressure and peripheral resistance. *J. Clin. Invest.* 27:290-298, 1948.

[53] GRINKER, R. R., KORCHIN, S. J., BASOWITZ, H., HAMBURG, D. A., SABSHIN, M., PERSKY, H., CHEVALIER, J. A., and BOARD, F. A.: A theoretical and experimental approach to problems of anxiety. *Arch. Neurol. and Psychiat. (Chicago)*, 76:420-431, Oct., 1956.

[54] GRINKER, R. R., and SPIEGEL, J. P.: *Men Under Stress.* Philadelphia, Blakiston, 1945; PERSKY, H., GRINKER, R. R., and GAMM, S.: Correlation between fluctuation of free anxiety and quantity of hippuric acid excretion. *Psychosom. Med., 14*:1, 1952; BASOWITZ, H., PERSKY, H., KORCHIN, S. J., and GRINKER, R. R.: *Anxiety and Stress.* New York. Blakiston, 1955.

[55] PERSKY, H., GRINKER, R. R., HAMBURG, D. A., SABSHIN, M. A., KORCHIN, S. J., BASOWITZ, H., and CHEVALIER, J. A.: Adrenal cortical function in anxious human subjects. *Arch. Neurol. and Psychiat. (Chicago)*, 76:549-558, Nov., 1956. A third article of this series concerns anxiety-producing interviews, terminating in the state-

metabolites: They found the twenty-four-hour urinary excretion of phenylhydrazine-reacting substances (hydroxycorticoids) on the base-day in anxious subjects 70 percent greater than in normal controls. For increased anxiety arousal, they resorted to "stress interviews," but no significant increase resulted.

According to Persky et al.: "Anxious subjects produce more hydrocortisone and metabolize it differently than normal subjects."[56] The increased production of hydrocortisone by the anxious individual has been demonstrated by such criteria as an elevated plasma hydrocortisone level,[57, 58] an elevated urinary hydroxycorticoid[59] and 17-ketosteroid excretion,[60] a greater urinary hydroxycorticoid output in response to exogenous corticotropin,[61] and an increased turnover of radioactivity-tagged hydrocortisone.[62] The altered metabolism of hydroxycortisone in the anxious subject is reflected in the greater proportion of 17-keto-

---

ment: "Our results highlight difficulties encountered in making the anxiety-stimulus interview effective, in controlling its severity, and in quantifying it in a life situation." Amen! GRINKER, R. R., SABSHIN, M., HAMBURG, D. A., BOARD, F. A., BASOWITZ, H., KORCHIN, S. J., PERSKY, H., and CHEVALIER, J. A.: The use of an anxiety-producing interview and its meaning to the subject. Arch. Neurol. and Psychiat. (Chicago), 77:406-419, April, 1957.

[56] PERSKY, H., MAROC, J., CONRAD, E., and BREEIJEN, A. D.: Blood corticotropin and adrenal weight-maintenance factor levels of anxious patients and normal subjects. Psychosom. Med., 21:379-386, Sept.-Oct., 1959.

[57] PERSKY, H., GRINKER, R. R., HAMBURG, D. A., SABSHIN, M., KORCHIN, S. J., BASOWITZ, H., and CHEVALIER, J. A.: Adrenal cortical function in anxious human subjects. Arch. Neurol. and Psychiat. (Chicago), 76:549, 1956.

[58] PERSKY, H., GROSZ, H. J., NORTON, J. A., and McMURTRY, M.: Effect of hypnotically-induced anxiety on the plasma hydrocortisone level of normal subjects. J. Clin. Endocr. 19:700, 1959.

[59] PERSKY, H., KORCHIN, S. J., BASOWITZ, H., BOARD, F. A., SABSHIN, M., HAMBURG, D. A., and GRINKER, R. R.: Effect of two psychological stresses on adrenocortical function: Studies on anxious and normal subjects. Arch. Neurol. and Psychiat. (Chicago), 81:219, 1959.

[60] HOWARD, J. M., OLNEY, J. M., FRAWLEY, J. P., PETERSON, R. E., SMITH, L. H., DAVIS, J. H., GUERRA, S., and DIBRELL, W. H.: Studies of adrenal function in combat and wounded soldiers. Ann. Surg., 141:314, 1955.

[61] PERSKY, H.: Adrenal cortical function in anxious human subjects: Effect of corticotropin (ACTH) on plasma hydrocortisone and urinary hydroxycorticoid excretion. Arch. Neurol. and Psychiat. (Chicago), 78:95, 1957.

[62] PERSKY, H.: Unpublished data.

steroids[63] and lesser proportion of hydroxycorticoids[64] relative to all the urinary metabolites of hydrocortisone following an exogenous dose of hydrocortisone." These investigators found that anxious patients have a mean plasma level of a newly identified corticoptropic substance which they label AWMF, more than twice that of a group of normal, encorticoid subjects. ACTH, however, is not significantly higher.

Maas *et al.* found no significant relationship between the rate of oxidation of DPP (N_1N-dimethyl-p-phenylenediamine) and the level of free anxiety. Plasma ascorbic acid values were found lower for all subgroups of their anxious patients, but the statistical difference was not significant. Serum copper levels were not different in the anxious compared with the non-anxious group.[65]

Recapitulation

In the present chapter we have outlined, however briefly and inadequately, investigations on emotional behavior. Many of them have been carried out with acumen and brilliance. We have witnessed the emergence of the limbic lobe, including the hypothalamus, assuming increasing stature in the theory of emotion.

Withal, however, we end this list of diverse investigations with the impression of many precious beads but no string. Nothing binds the results together in satisfying order; there is insufficiency of unifying concepts.

One reason for this, according to the present thesis, is failure to realize that the action of nerve centers is meaningless if considered apart from their peripheral action and function. While neuromuscular and other peripheral structures are brought into the picture now and then in the investigations recounted above, a balanced view of their relationships and significance is conspicuously lacking. We are misled to consider muscular tension

[63] ELMADJIAN, F.: Adrenocortical function of combat infantrymen in Korea. *Ciba Foundation Coll. Endocr.* 8:627, 1955.

[64] PERSKY, H.: Adrenocortical function in anxious human subjects: The disappearance of hydrocortisone from plasma and its metabolic fate. *J. Clin. Endocr.* 17:760, 1957.

[65] MAAS, J. W., GLESER, G. C., and GOTTSCHALK, L. A.: Schizophrenia, anxiety, and biochemical factors. *Arch. Gen. Psychiat. (Chicago),* 4:109-118, Feb., 1961.

states as one group among many others of less, equal or greater importance in emotional behavior. It is as if we had been reading an account of the telephone system of the United States, replete with details of central stations, but making relatively little mention of the use and significance of the millions of telephones employed by users. Has the science of emotional behavior lost its way in a maze of detail?

Not altogether. In the following chapters I shall try to show that there is a way out of the woods.

Emotional Behavior Defined

Meanwhile, a unifying conception may help us to assimilate the contents of this chapter. *It seems warranted to distinguish behavior as emotional by the presence of markedly increased integrated response in both the vegetative and cerebrospinal systems but with the former generally more evident.*[66]

A practical moral follows for doctors and clinical psychologists. If they are to be good therapists, showing their patients how to attain the emotional security they seek, they will need know-how based on sound psychology and physiology. Otherwise, therapy will continue to fall prey to undue influence of ideologies, and their patients will continue to long for the relief they fail to secure, except temporarily and unsatisfactorily from sedatives and tranquilizers.

---

[66] Conditions of fever, epilepsy and other disease frequently show increased excitation in both branches likewise, but the response is obviously disordered and without appearance of the integrated effort that characterizes emotion.

Chapter IV

INTERNAL COMMUNICATION

THE KEY TO BEHAVIOR

Each person has a code by which he lives. The code is not a secret one, but is private and highly individuated. To interpret it requires the person himself. In this respect it differs from what are generally known as codes—for example, the Morse code, which is in common use by telegraphers. However, the difference is not complete. People of the same culture and era tend to have codes with much in common, particularly if they can see and hear and smell and taste and if they have at least fairly healthy muscles. Even so, their private codes differ from one another no less than their thumbprints. Accordingly, there are differences but also important similarities.

Among the many important characteristics of his own being which man has largely overlooked or neglected is the internal code of which I speak. It might as well be called the *internal language* which each human being develops as he grows older. Without this internal language, man would not move and have his being. Just as the life of humanity requires means of communication between each individual and others, if there is to be a collective life, so also there is continual dependency in every person upon means of internal communication.[1]

---

[1] References to the internal "code'" are becoming more frequent in neurophysiology. For example, Granit obtained registrations from the optic tract upon stimulating the retina adequately, demonstrating that both frequency and pattern are important. This led Ulf Söderberg to comment: "That is of course an example of a code within the central nervous system, for the retina is a part of that system and the optic tract is a tract within the central nervous system" (SÖDERBERG, ULF: in JASPER, H. H., *et al.* [Eds.]: *Reticular Formation of the Brain*, New York, Little, 1958, p. 110).

Internal communication is based upon the occurrence of signals in the

54

From each and every organ and tissue of his body come incessant signals in simultaneous and successive patterns. The signals plus his interpretations constitute his degree of awareness of the inner state of his being and of the outer world. Without these signals he would be isolated from both. Without them life would be meaningless. With them, to some extent, he represents what is without and what is within, but often he fails to differentiate clearly.

Signals from within enable him grossly to say, "I feel well!" or "I feel ill!" and often to designate localities in which they arise. As will be outlined hereinafter, signals from the visceral organs are part and parcel of his evaluating system, disorders of which occur in every psychoneurosis.

Signals Are of Two Kinds

The internal code of which I speak includes two classes of signals. (a) The first kind have long been familiar to experimental psychologists as (i) sensations or as (ii) gestalt forms. Sensations are conscious signals, which may be apprehended as conscious or may be overlooked. Much that is conscious in us is nevertheless overlooked, unperceived. (b) The second kind are signals which trigger operations of the organism, through associative or motor sections of the nervous system. These signals may not be conscious. There is no type of signals analogous to these in the telephone system, except the ringing of bells and the like. Computer systems, however, abound in signals of Type (b) as well as of Type (a). In the present volume we shall call signals of both kinds *automatic controls*. As will be set forth later our patients are to learn to distinguish from these the voluntary neuromuscular controls.

Internal Communications System

For his use in communications man is endowed with a system composed of an estimated ten billion amplifier cells in his brain,

---

nervous system. The account in the present chapter is general only. An important contribution to the theory of this field has been made by A. M. Uttley. (UTTLEY, A. M.: The classification of signals in the nervous system. *Electroenceph. Clin. Neurophysiol.*, VI (3):479-494, Aug., 1954).

and by these structures and the networks of nerve fibers which are the counterparts of telephone or telegraph wires he can communicate within himself in a manner which is essential for his every act.[2] The system, if not as large, is comparable in the number of amplifiers and wires with that of the telephone circuits of the entire United States, which it greatly exceeds in intricacy.

Knowledge of the structures of the cells and fibers in this system has been the aim of neuroanatomists for many decades and notable progress has been recorded. The function of these structures has been the subject of investigations by hundreds of neurophysiologists all over the civilized world. Among special journals devoted to these fields are the *Journal of Neurophysiology* and the *Journal of Electroencephalography and Clinical Neurophysiology*.

Each individual, then, is endowed with a structure for self-communication of vast extent and intricacy. But its use depends upon his own development and indeed constitutes the basis of what most of us are prone to regard as education of each individual.

Extensive study by thousands of scientists has yielded a large body of knowledge about the anatomy and physiology of the brain and nervous system. It is only one particular use, namely, as internal language or code of individual being, which has received relatively little attention.

Introspective Psychology

Introspective psychologists have described certain phases of our internal language without using this terminology, and a few have given them careful laboratory investigation under various names and under various conceptions differing extensively from the present one which I am endeavoring to unfold. Toward the end of the nineteenth century and until the advent of World War I, the German experimental psychologists made history in the field which I prefer to term *autosensory examination*. Psychologists of Britain, France, America and other advanced countries

---

[2] McCulloch, Warren S.: The brain as a computing machine. *Electrical Engineering,* June, 1949.

likewise made significant contributions. Among the Germans, Wilhelm Wundt[3] early appeared as the leader, while William James[4] made striking advances among Americans. The Wuerzberger of school of psychologists began studies on the processes of thinking.[5]

All their findings and those of many others contributed much to our knowledge of inner observation. However, I believe that a still greater value and utility can eventually result if we more clearly apprehend and investigate what is here called internal communication or code or language.

Frankly, upon examining the protocol of introspective reports published from most laboratories, I am amazed at their lack of clarity on the fundamental point of this chapter, that every person has a code of his own with individual differences, which he could be taught to observe and to distinguish from meaning. Mankind is familiar with many other kinds of codes, of which, as said above, the Morse code is one familiar example. Precisely the difference between code sounds of the telegrapher's key, the dots and dashes of the records, from the meanings is the most significant feature of any code, including that which every individual employs internally. However, this difference did not occur clearly to experimental psychologists until 1911, upon the publication of my own study, entitled "On Meaning and Understanding."[6] *Today, upon examining even the most outstanding publications of introspective reports, including those of the Wuerzberger*

---

[3] WUNDT, WILHELM: *Grundzüge der Physiologischen Psychologie.* Leipzig, Wilhelm Engelmann, Vol. 1, 1908, Vol. 2, 1910, Vol. 3, 1911.

[4] JAMES, WILLIAM: The Principles of Psychology. New York, Henry Holt & Co., 1907. Vol. II.

[5] WATT, H. J.: Experimentelle Beiträge zu einer Theorie des Denkens. *Arch. f.d. ges. Psychol.* 4:312-368, 1905; Literaturbericht. *Ibid.,* 7:42, 44, 47, 1906; MESSER, A.: Experimentelle-psychologische Untersuchungen über das Denken. *Arch. f.d. ges. Psychol.,* 8:68, 1906; BÜHLER, K.: Tatsachen und Probleme zu einer Psychologie der Denkvorgänge, i. Ueber Gedanken. *Arch. f.d. ges. Psychol.,* 9:352, 363, 1907; ACH, N.: Ueber die Willenstätigkeit und das Denken: eine experimentelle Untersuchung mit einem Anhange über das Hippsche Chronoskop, 1905; WUNDT, W.: Ueber Ausfragexperimente und über die Methoden zur Psychologie des Denkens. *Psychol. Stud.* 3:334, 1907.

[6] JACOBSON, EDMUND: On meaning and understanding. *Amer. J. Psychol.,* 22: 553-557, Oct., 1911.

school, we still miss a clear-cut apprehension that there are continual internal sensory and imaginal code signals which need to be distinguished from the meanings. These signals plus their meanings constitute what we call our psychic lives.

To understand what really goes on in the mind, technical autosensory examination is taught until subjects become experienced observers.

Watson on Behaviorism

As is known, with the aid of Carl Lashley, J. B. Watson cast doubt upon the scientific validity of psychological introspective methods.[7] Accordingly, he founded what is called *behaviorism.* The positive aspects of this branch have been highly productive, particularly in animal research.

Watson was said to claim that my own objective recordings and direct measurements of mental activity, first published in 1927, confirmed his theory that thinking is largely a laryngeal process. However, what I really was able to establish objectively for the first time was that miniscule use of the speech apparatus is characteristic in thinking. Clearly, to conclude from this that I found thinking largely a laryngeal function would be a gross misstatement. Without doubt, as I showed, mechanisms of internal speech are part and parcel of the thinking process, but ocular images and tensions are no less common. Indeed, the whole neuromuscular system plays an integral part.

Watson Neglected Controlled Introspective Report

Furthermore, contrary to the theory of Watson, my findings owed their very genesis to carefully controlled introspective protocol from observers whom I trained technically—a training and experience which Watson lacked and minimized. It was precisely the introspectively observed signals which led me to realize that reflection, memory, imagination, fantasy and other forms of mental activity probably are a function of neuromuscular activity everywhere in the organism and not of brain activity alone. Thus

---

[7] WATSON, J. B.: *Behaviorism.* New York, Norton, 1924.

I sought to develop electrophysiological means of objective identification and of recording of precisely those difficult-to-observe
internal procedures of thinking and of other forms of mental
activity. It was necessary for me to devise apparatus of necessary
delicacy, which at first appeared impossible to my engineering
colleagues. The features of this search have been published, but
will be recounted more adequately in a forthcoming volume entitled *The Science of Physiological Psychiatry.*

Historical Controversy Over Imageless Thought

Looking backward to the era when controversy flourished over
the existence or not of *imageless thought,* we can now offer definite answers. In the daily studies performed over past decades in
this laboratory and clinic, numerous subjects have received technical training and their reports have been secured in unprece-
dented numbers. We are led to believe that much of the imagery
and muscular tension patterns employed constantly in our psychic
lives are of extremely rapid, faint, vague and transient character.
Only with the incessant daily drill of many years, rather than in
the briefer studies of most psychological laboratories, does the
skill develop really to discern the fainter and more transient of
these signals. Evidently, thinking is never imageless.

In various publications and volumes in the field of experimental
psychology, my findings on the electrophysiology of mental activities have been said to support a *motor theory* of thinking. *No
such intention or interpretation* appears in my own publications.
As said above, over the years of autosensory observations, there
has been abundant evidence that the sensory and imaginal signals
as well as the motor play in each and every form of mental activity investigated, including every emotion as well as attention,
perception, recall, reflection and fantasy. From the wealth of
data secured over more than three decades of controlled investigations, it seems safe to assume that the present investigations
have led successfully not to a theory of thinking but to a firm
knowledge of many of the basic physiologic and psychologic
characteristics of what is known as mental activities. On this
understanding, together with common principles previously de-

veloped by other psychologists, we propose to base a new but scientific physiological psychology and psychiatry.

Controlled Internal Observation Can be Both Scientific and Practical

The results can prove of great theoretical as well as of practical importance. Our understanding of man's continual representation of changing external and internal stimuli can be increased and can be put to practical use in daily living. This will require the distribution of knowledge and skills gained from our scientific endeavors to the public through educative channels. The purposes can be medical training and prophylaxis; but also they can apply in general education.

One subject in which man may become educated to his theoretical and practical advantage concerns his daily efforts for success. Through his internal code he can learn to observe when and where he is making efforts and to count the costs. He can learn to govern his exertions with an eye to economy. In engineering terms, this can mean *increased efficiency*.

Chapter V

EFFORT COSTS AND ACCOMPLISHMENTS

SECTION A—WHEREFORE?

Life a Succession of Efforts

THE LIFE of man is a succession of efforts. In lower forms of life also we see evidences of striving for nutrition and other ends necessary for survival. However primitive the function of seeking, we confidently assume that it always has a chemical aspect. From the chemical aspect we are learning something especially about the complexity of the protein molecules which enter into the constitution of living matter. From the psychological aspect we can consider the goals which the life of organisms illustrates at every moment.

Goals

Perhaps we can gain a better understanding of certain goals of man if once more we recall lower forms of animal life. Any one-cell organism, such as the amoeba, will serve as an example. Under the microscope we observe the procedure that ensues when a particle which can prove nutritious is approached. The cytoplasm of the protozoan flows about the substance until it is totally surrounded. Digestion and assimilation follow. Thus, in the one-cell organism, processes occur of irritability, locomotion, inhibition, digestion and assimilation. Evolutionists have described how these and other chief functions of the cell become modified in the ascending scale of animal life. Cells become specialized in function and tend to replace the primitive "general practitioner" cells. Tissues arise which tend to serve a special function. Finally there develops the differentiated organism composed of myriads of specialized cells in specialized tissues,

61

many of which are in specialized organs. The specialization is not only in the locale and in the chemistry of the cells, tissues and organs; it is also in their goals or functions. In higher animals each specialized cell has become so modified that it subserves certain functions of the total organism, but without entirely losing the primitive functions of irritability, inhibition, digestion and assimilation. If these functions are lost, the cell or tissue or organ which suffers the loss becomes necrotic. Life passes.

The goal of the amoeba which engulfs the nutritious particle can be stated objectively. As previously stated, we do not know if in any sense, however primitive, the goal can be properly said to be conscious. With this understanding we can define the term biologically. Literally, it is the *end* of the action of the cell, the result of which is nutrition and survival. Biologists might call it *adjustment to environment* or might use some other complex phrase. For medical purposes I would suggest the simple phrase *adaptive success* or *successful reaction* or shorten it to the single word, *success* or *welfare*.

Goal Success

In any objective sense, *success* or *welfare* in one respect or another is the goal of each moment of the life of every organism, be it amoeba or be it man himself. Whatever are the trophic or other physical forces that lead the amoeba to approach its food or at times to withdraw from noxious elements in the environment, it would seem reasonable to assume that, through some manner or process such as the tendency to approach or to withdraw, there often is representation in the cell or in the more complex organism of the favorable or unfavorable aspects of such elements. So far as the response of the amoeba is autogenous and not forced upon it, we can assume that the response is conditioned by some form of representation, however primitive.

However this may be, we are fully aware that in higher animals there exist such representative functions in plenty. The household dog or cat furnishes many illustrations such as the smelling of food or the cringing or the running away at the threat of punishment. Animals, like man, manifest desires or fears, and these obviously are representative processes having to do with goals of *success* or of *welfare*.

Universality of the WSA Response

Evidently, on every scale of development the animal organism responds not to the whole environment but to that portion as a rule which concerns its welfare. The response always is *selective*. This means only that the response of any organism at every moment tends to be selective in what aspects of the environment are sensed or signalled. In short, be it amoeba or be it man, there occurs in the organism a certain selection to which the response is so far as possible adapted. Expressing all of this in a phrase, we can say that the welfare-selective-adaptive response is universal in animaldom. In man various cells, tissues and organs have become specialized to carry out this response.

Goals and Muscle Contraction

In the process of evolution, accordingly, the performance of locomotion and of all other movement tends to become limited to and specialized in one tissue, namely, in muscle. Muscle fibers produce motion in accordance with their location, their course, their origin and their insertion. When muscle fibers contract, there is always a goal or end. It has been shown by Hoffmann that reflexes, which to earlier physiologists often appeared purposeless, really subserve functions of orderly and coordinated movement and that the reflex connections are prerequisite.[1]

It is important for practitioners to realize that human muscles subserve various functions in addition to locomotion and exercise. Smooth muscles, among other functions, contract and relax for purposes of digestion, blood circulation and blood pressure, the conduct of urine and the secretion and excretion of glandular products. Cardiac muscles contract and relax for their pumping action. Striated muscles, in addition to the goals of locomotion and of movements of the limbs and of other parts of the organism, play a chief role in our every effort.

---

[1] HOFFMANN, PAUL: *Untersuchungen über die Eigenreflexe (Sehnenreflexe) Menschlicher Muskeln.* Berlin, Julius Springer, 1922.

Neglect of the Role of Effort

In an advancing science of man, the role of effort warrants increasing attention, yet our own laboratory and clinic is approximately the only institution which has consistently specialized in this field. As indicated, we find effort indissolubly associated with patterns of muscular contraction. It is well known that approximately half the weight of the human body is due to muscle; approximately half the free and bound water of the body is in muscle fibers and in the interstitial fluid in muscle; while the heat production of the body is due largely to muscular contraction and relaxation and therefore also the body temperature, except insofar as this is under nervous and perhaps glandular control.

These are some of the basic mechanics of muscle and thus of effort, but we are brought to the entrance of a much neglected subsidiary topic: muscular, therefore human, efficiency:

Human Muscle Inefficiency

Under normal environmental conditions, their mechanical efficiency is only 20 to 30 per cent. From this it follows, as pointed out by Suggs and Splinter,[2] that for a given quantity of energy to be expended as work, two to four times as much energy must be dissipated as heat if body temperature is not to increase.[3]

Excessive Anxiety is One Example of Inefficiency

Since human effort efficiency thus is relatively low as compared with the best of machines constructed up to date, new methods

---

[2] Suggs, C. W., and Splinter, W. E.: Some physiologic responses of man to workload and environment. *J. Appl. Physiol.*, *16*(3):413, May, 1961.

[3] These writers continue: "Therefore, part of the response accompanying exercise or work is due to the increased activity of the heat-dissipating mechanism. For this reason the physiological responses to workload are closely related to thermal stresses (Belding, H. S., and Hatch, T. F.: *Trans. Amer. Soc. Heating Air-Conditioning Engrs.*, 62:213, 1956) in the derivation of an index for evaluating heat stress in terms of resulting physiological strains, effectively included workload as a thermal stress. Their index of heat stress consists of the ratio (100) E req./E max. The sum of the heat produced, the radiative gain and the convective gain, E req., is the evaporation required to prevent an increase in body temperature. E max. is the maximum amount of evaporation from the body permitted by the environment."

of study are needed to shore up our strivings. Excessive emotional tension is one example of human energy waste.

Behavior is a Function of Muscles

On the role of muscle contraction, J. L. Conel writes significantly: "Sufficient evidence has been accumulated to prove that the voluntary contraction, relaxation, and co-ordination of striated muscles in the human body is a function of the cerebral cortex. All behavior, including morals, is on last analysis the use of muscles. Behavior undergoes development with advancing age and training in the use of the muscles, and the quality of morals in behavior enters when the individual voluntarily directs the use of his muscles for benefit or harm to himself and other humans. Development of the moral element in behavior is well under way at the age of twenty-four months in training the infant to control excitation, inhibition, and co-ordination of his muscles in such acts as sucking his thumb, crying, demanding the center of attention, sharing his toys with other infants or grabbing their property from them, suppressing tantrums, the elimination of excreta, and in many other acts which have a social bearing."[4]

Brain not Overlooked

In thus emphasizing the role of muscle in the life of higher organisms, I may seem to be overlooking the part played by the nervous system, including the brain, but I am not. To each muscle, as every doctor knows, belong an afferent and an efferent supply of nerves. When the muscle is in action, the peripheral nerves likewise are in action, just as when we use a telephone transmitter or receiver, not only the mouthpiece and the earpiece are in action but also the incoming and outgoing wires.

At the moment of each and every effort in animals and in man, contraction of some muscle fibers and relaxation in others occurs indispensably. This said, we can add that in the intact animal, not only is there appropriate simultaneous action in the peripheral nerve supply but in certain sections of the spinal cord, medulla

---

[4] CONEL, J. L.: *The Postnatal Development of the Human Cerebral Cortex. 6. The Cortex of the Twenty-Four Month Infant* Cambridge, Harvard, 1959, p. 275.

and brain as well. This is not all. The cardiovascular system tends to participate in every effort because of the necessity of oxygen and of other supplies to the contracting muscle and also because of the necessity of the removal of carbon dioxide and of other waste products. Presumably for sustained muscular contraction in our efforts, also one or another portion of the glandular system of internal secretion tends to participate. Much remains to be investigated.[5]

The Effort Circuit

The smooth muscle of the gastrointestinal system tends to participate in the *effort circuit*, as I shall call it hereafter. In conditions of anger, fear, hostility and other violent emotions, my teacher, Walter Cannon, was among the first to show that digestive activity tended to become inhibited.[6] Psychiatrists are well aware of gastrointestinal symptoms in their patients suffering from acute and chronic emotional states. As we shall see upon investigation, emotional states always involve states of effort.

Every school of psychiatric thought and every division of opinion in each school will need to seek bases in the fundamentals of physiological psychiatry. We can give the following example to illustrate a beginning toward this end by psychoanalysts. In a lucid account of the "nature of symptoms," Chapter 1 of *Neurosis and Psychosis*, Beula Chamberlain Bosselman begins her volume as follows: "The disorders of function known as neurosis and psychosis represent relatively inefficient and unrealistic attempts on the part of the individual to establish intrapersonal and interpersonal integration under difficult circumstances. The individuals's symptoms are the expressions of his *striving* [italics mine] for reconciliation of diverse elements within himself, as well as his *striving* for compromise with the demands of the outer world."[7]

The physiologist likewise is led to find the basis of neurosis and

---

[5] SCHWARTZ, N. B., and LEIN, A.: Effects of thyroxin on skeletal muscle function. *Amer. J. Physiol., 182*(1):5-11, 1955.

[6] CANNON, W. B.: *Bodily Changes in Pain, Hunger, Fear and Rage.* New York, Appleton, 2nd ed., 1929.

[7] BOSSELMAN, B. C.: *Neurosis and Psychosis.* Springfield, Thomas, 1956, 2nd ed., Chapters 3, 6.

psychosis to a large extent in *striving*. He objects only when this term is used vaguely, and prefers that it be given definite, precise meaning. If *striving* is anything more than a meaningless abstraction, it must refer to a definite kind of process within the human organism. As such, presumably it will include certain activity within the brain which can not yet be delineated. It lies close at hand to see that Bosselman's use of the term *striving* is not far removed from what is delineated as *effort* in the present volume.

If psychoanalysts are aided by explaining some of their theories in terms of basic physiology, it may prove useful to them to substitute the term *striving* for *effort* as employed in the present monograph. As a definite process in the human organism identifiable physiologically at a particular moment of time, all striving, like all effort, will be marked by specific patterns of neuromuscular tension-contraction.

Tension Defined

What has been said about striving will hold likewise for another synonym of effort, namely, *tension*. By tension I mean muscular contraction. By an extension of the term, according to context, it may indicate (a) the accompanying physiological state or (b) excessive muscular contraction, as when we speak of "tense persons."[8] As employed by analysts, the term *tension* often lacks precision.[9] They may be aided, I hope, if they will bear in mind

---

[8] Then the term is used to mean the same as "neuromuscular hypertension," not necessarily referring to increased blood pressure. The word "hypertension", referring only to the muscle and nervous state, is coming into wider usage.

[9] Sometimes it refers to painful experience. Thus Freud: "In the psycho-analytical theory of the mind we take it for granted that the course of mental processes is automatically regulated by 'the pleasure principle': that is to say, we believe that any given process originates in an unpleasant state of tension and thereupon determines for itself such a path that its ultimate issue coincides with a relaxation of this tension, i.e., with avoidance of 'pain' or with production of pleasure" FREUD, S.: *Beyond the Pleasure Principle*, [Hubback, C. J. M. (Trans)]. New York, Boni and Liveright, p. 1. We gain the impression that the resolution of states of tension is experienced as pleasure (p. 82). Possibly here Freud refers to the hypertension of anxiety; if so, resolution is attended by feelings of relief rather than "pleasure." Freud's statement that pleasure "corresponds" with a decrease of "the quantity of excitation present in the psychic life" (*loc. cit.*, p. 2) is not confirmed in electroneuromyometric physiology. Action-potential levels increase in states of pleasure as well as of pain.

that to be a concrete occurrence in the human organism, the term *tension*, like *striving* and *effort*, must in the last analysis refer to patterns of neuromuscular tension-contraction of the physiologist.

Effort Involves the Whole Organism

Thus, in this brief review, we begin to realize that our every effort includes and involves each system of the entire organism. Certainly, effort is not limited to muscle alone, but while the participation of any other system of the body may require investigation, it is certain that the participation of the nervous and muscular system is essential in effort.

When addressing physiologists I have at times explained why I have specialized in the investigation of muscular contraction in human and animal activities. I have answered the self-imposed question by saying that muscle is the one tissue which is observably in action during effort-activity of the whole organism and of its chief portions and which can be conveniently identified and subjected to quantitative methods and recording. I hope that psychiatrists will bear this in mind also.

Proprioceptive Signals

When muscles contract during effort, the intact human being in whom this occurs experiences certain signals which belong to the inner code discussed in the foregoing chapter. These signals originate in sensory end-organs both in the muscles themselves and in other moving parts. Ordinarily the individual does not recognize these signals as such. He knows that his arm moves when he experiences the signals mentioned, but he does not distinguish and differentiate the signals as such as do telegraphers in deciphering the Morse code. He does not and need not know that he has muscle sensations which arise in muscle spindles.

Nevertheless, we can say that in man the signals or sensations mentioned are conscious. For we know that if these sensations are notably lacking, as in the legs in *tabes dorsalis*, the patient fails to use the parts in normal, healthy dexterity. He shows *stamping gait*. Similarly, if these sensations are lacking as in nerve trauma, the part affected may not be used with normal skill.

Sensation Differs from Awareness (Perception)

Accordingly, we can say that the signals or sensations of which we have been writing are conscious sensations, even though the individual is not aware of them as such. Thus we draw the distinction between a subjective process which is conscious, but of which we are not aware, from one of which we have become aware. Often it is necessary to cultivate such awareness. This consists in teaching the individual to observe his autosensory states. Such teaching, I believe, is basic to psychiatry. It is the key to the application of the methods of progressive relaxation and of self-operations control.

The distinction between sensation which ipso facto is conscious and the recognition that this sensation is present will serve to clear up some of the obscurity in current theories of the unconscious. We may be unaware (and in this sense unconscious) that we have a certain sensation, although this is conscious.

When the individual learns to distinguish the signal or sensation present in muscle contraction and to locate it, he can note that the muscle-sense presents him with an internal representation which constantly changes according to his each and every effort. No such sensation or signal originates in or emanates directly from the brain and nervous system, although they participate likewise in the effort-circuit. Therefore, *for purposes of control*, we train the patient to become expert in identifying the loci and transient patterns of his effort-tensions, subjectively aroused upon stretch of muscle spindles when muscle fibers shorten.

Thereby he becomes educated toward counting the costs of his efforts. We shall see how this can prepare for emotional control.

Effort-Tension Costs

Man is endowed with structures of inestimable value for his daily efforts, if he will but take advantage of their presence and learn to utilize them. When muscle contracts, as it does at each moment of his striving, an internal signal system operates which can apprize him in a gross manner, at least, of the cost. Muscle tension, as we know, is registered at each instant by the muscle-sense of Bell, but commonly passes ignored, unless the individual learns to identify the specific sensation. This requires *training* as in any other technical art or science.

No instrument with many parts has been constructed by man supplied with devices to indicate the energy expenditure, however grossly, in each of its parts. Yet such devices are part and parcel of the sensory action of the muscle spindles which register in each and every effort. The amount of time which many individuals allot to golf or to other games or avocations, if devoted to the cultivation of the muscle-sense, could prove an aid to increase their ability toward increased daily efficiency, including emotional control, as will be indicated in the following pages.[10]

If every effort tension has an energy-cost, it behooves scientific mankind to have ordered knowledge thereof on which to base a practical economy of living. Commonly, industrial man employs energies excessively and unnecessarily in his each and every pursuit, including his diversions. Excessive use of any apparatus, according to common knowledge, brings disrepair and premature decay. Can it be otherwise with excessive use of the human apparatus? It is not reasonable to suppose so. On the contrary, our current civilization abounds with individual examples of excessive tension in living: We are beset with peptic ulcer, spastic colon and esophagus, arterial hypertension, coronary heart disasters, fatigue states, functional or psychosomatic disorders of varied types, neuroses and psychoneuroses, and countless other varieties of tension disorders. In consequence, we can assume there is much pathologic wear and tear on vital organs. These are some of the costs of hypertensive living.

SECTION B—WHY?

Necessity of Neuromuscular Effort

Not only when man faces stress but also at every other moment there is reaction to continual change occurring both external and internal to him. The fortress of life is always under siege. Persistent objective security is never attained. Change must be met with change. Homeostasis and other internal balances must be

---

[10] JACOBSON, E., *Anxiety and Tension Control*. Philadelphia, Lippincott, 1964.

maintained at the cost of the energy required by countless mechanical controls, responding to ceaseless volleys of internal signals. Externally, the effort-tension system needs to be alert, except in deep sleep in preparation for the coming day.

Neuromusclar Effort Accomplishes Representation and Interpretation of Meanings

What is the manner and what is the goal of human striving which occurs thus incessantly in life? What does man do and why? The answer requires us to review what was said in a preceding chapter. It is hoped that the reader will be indulgent, recalling that exposition often becomes clearer upon repetition.

1. To some extent, man registers by his internal signal system what is occurring without and within him: He looks, listens, smells, tastes, notes sensations from the muscles, joints and viscera of tactile, pain, pressure and other modalities. While the sensations are conscious, however dimly, he does not become distinctly aware of them as such. Appropriately we might call the operational system of sensation-signals *automatic autocommunication unawares*. What is sensed, however consciously, is not necessary perceived. Perception denotes the advent of meaning. This occurs upon neuromuscular intervention by what are appropriately called *designation processes*.[11]

Neuromuscular Effort Enters into Every Moment of Perception

Accordingly, the very act of perception includes neuromuscular reaction in addition to the neuromuscular action necessary for vision, hearing or other sensory act. In agreement therewith are B. Brouwer's findings in his study entitled "Centrifugal Influence on Centripetal Systems in the Brain."[12] In this investigator's words: "We accept that there is also a centrifugal side in the process of vision, of hearing, and so on. I believe that a further analysis of these descending tracts to pure sensory centers will

---

[11] JACOBSON, E.: On meaning and understanding. *Amer. J. Psychol.*, 22:553-577, Oct., 1911.

[12] BROUWER, B.: Centrifugal influence on centripetal systems in the brain. *J. Nerv. Ment. Dis.*, 77:621, 1933.

also help physiologists and psychologists to understand some of their experiences."[12] In attention, according to Livingston, descending projections make the lower sensory pathways more receptive. Livingston continues: "To my mind the real beginnings of a new understanding of sensory mechanisms commenced with the discovery . . . that an important muscle sense organ, the muscle-spindle, could be controlled by a number of central nervous structures.[13]

Control of Spindle Signals

"This control was exercised by activating or depressing the small motor horn cells which had already been shown to govern the rate of discharge of spindle afferents."[14] Livingston cites further evidence leading to the conclusion: "Thus every sensory circuit within spinal levels has been found to be vulnerable to influence from higher centers."

Within the Limitations of Human Representation and Reaction

As previously stated, man does not react to the total of reality but only to that section of reality to which his senses are attuned. His apprehension of reality is further limited by his attention to what he regards as important at any moment of reaction, a *selectivity* which is in turn a function of his memory and emotional responses.

These extremely complex functions are complicated further by his state of cerebral and neuromuscular excitability at the moment of apprehension—a state which varies greatly both generally and locally. It runs high in emotional reactions; we say that the individual shows high residual tensions.

The Human Mind Acts Like a Microscope

Under all these diverse forms of limitation, the mind of man acts more like a microscope than a telescope. It magnifies only

---

[13] LIVINGSTON, R. H.: In JASPER, H. H., *et al.* (Eds): *Central Control of Afferent Activity in Reticular Formation of the Brain,* New York, Little, 1958, pp. 177-185.

[14] GRANIT, R., and KAADA, B. R.: Influence of stimulation of central nervous structures on muscle spindles in cat. *Acta Physiol. Scand.* 27:130, 1952; GRANIT, R.: *Receptors and Sensory Perception.* New Haven, Yale, 1955.

within a short range of his highly selected experience, which in turn reflects only a highly selected section of temporal and spatial reality. Furthermore, his mind acts more like a camera taking snapshots of reality than a moving picture. His visual representations, which constitute much of his filing system of life, are, to a large extent, static, like snapshots.

Concepts are Static as a Rule and are Subject to Errors not Realized

This is convenient, but often misleading. A snapshot offers only a time-abstraction or classification of reality. If mistaken for a fuller representation it fails to depict the constant change present in what is seen. Thus any concept of man, insofar as it is static, must fail to depict the changing character of the reality he faces. To date, the only concepts which successfully overcome this misinformation are those of calculus.

From what has been said it may be evident that people are prone to trust their impressions far too much. Scientists and others can learn to allow for constant errors if they will realize the defects in their own apprehension devices. In a sense, man's every conception distorts reality. Most of all, the anxious person commonly fails to apprehend that the reality he depicts is far different from the reality he faces.

Neuromuscular Effort Accomplishes Evaluation

2. The organism evaluates. This complicated act has been subjected to scientific study much less than sensation and perception, discussed above. In Chapter VIII will be stated reasons for believing that the process of evaluation partially includes visceral reaction patterns. According to E. Gellhorn: "The evaluation of sensory experience by the frontal lobes is a prerequisite of an emotional arousal on a sensory basis."[15] Subjects trained to observe their own mental processes (autosensory observation) com-

---

[15] GELLHORN, E.: *Physiological Foundations of Neurology and Psychiatry.* U. of Minn., 1953, p. 356. He assumes that corticohypothalamic connections are restricted to the frontal lobe (WARD, A. A., JR., and McCULLOCH, W. S.: The projection of the frontal lobe on the hypothalamus. *J. Neurophysiol., 10*:309-314, 1947).

monly report evaluation in each experience. To realize what
evaluation means in his own experience, even the untrained observer has only to cross the street when there is heavy traffic. He
sees the approaching automobile not just as an object moving in
space but as a menace to his safety unless he judges accurately
its speed and his own. For further examples, the untrained observer has only to note his own experiences as he listens and
watches television productions.

Neuromuscular Effort Accomplishes Appropriate Response

3. To what he perceives and evaluates, the individual reacts
accordingly. Reaction includes the effort-circuit: In the instance
of the oncoming automobile, he hurries or stops or takes other
action. As employed in this volume, the effort-circuit is meant to
include not only the action of the peripheral unit, with muscular
contraction patterns and their inevitable concomitants in the
peripheral and central nervous system, but also the prerequisite
action of the cordiovascular and other organic systems.

Man's Effort Reaction (PET)

We can again say that it is important to realize that *perception,
evaluation and neuromuscular-tension reaction are not three successive events but on the contrary are inseparably intertwined in
our every moment of experience.* Our perceptions do not occur
as logical events separate from our reactions, but our reaction-
responses already are acting to color our perceptions. We are
already reacting when we perceive the oncoming car as dangerous, the oncoming animal as vicious, the oncoming person as
friendly, etc. In short, our reactions in part determine how and
what we perceive. The neurophysiology of this view has been
recounted from Livingston[16] (see Figs. 1 and 2, pp. 32 and 33).

In Anxiety This Response is Overwrought

In situations arousing anxiety, we assume that the evaluation
function can become protracted, accompanied by endless reflec-

---

[16] LIVINGSTON, *op. cit.*, pp. 177ff,

tion for problem solving. In anxiety neurosis, the reflection-evaluation becomes a drain on the subject's energy, often marked by insomnia, fatigue and other signs of tension disorder.[17]

RESUME

At every moment, as a rule, the organism reacts for survival, for security, for adaptation, for some success. I have called this the welfare response. This is as true of the one-celled protozoan as it is true of man. Much of the mechanism of this response is built into the cells, the intervening fluids and the interconnections. The response is in many respects automatic. As we go up the scale from the one-celled organism toward the primates, the automations become extremely complex. For example, they include the actions of the enzyme systems present in every cell. They include countless other mechanisms varying with each genus, species and individual organism. As higher animals become differentiated in their cells, tissue and organs, one tissue stands out at the disposal of the organism for its welfare response which is not on an automatic basis. This is the striated musculature with its intricate connections to the brain and other sections of the central and vegetative nervous system. The brain has been compared with central of the phone system. It is no less complicated perhaps than all of the central circuits of the United States together. In one respect it is far more complicated. In the telephone system as a whole, millions of messages pass simultaneously over the many wires. These messages are for the most

---

[17] Further on related neurophysiology, we quote from a contribution by J. Elkes: "What normally manifests, what finally is selected out, or as we say, what we 'experience' represents in fact, a final common path. Yet the activation of such an affective response, and the genetically programmed cell assembly which subserves it, is presumably preceded, within fractions of a second, by several simultaneous transactions involving the temporal apposition, convergence, and coding of neural patterns at widely separated topographical levels. It may, for example, involve the taking in of sensory cues (or the activation of a memory trace); the analysis and matching of these in terms of cognate traces, or, as we say, 'experience'; a regrouping and further condensation of these transforms in terms of their appetitive (YES) or aversive (NO) connotation; and the final activation of the appropriate motor-somato-endocrine response" (ELKES, J.: Drugs influencing affect and behavior: Possible neural correlates in relation to mode of action. In SIMON, A., et al. [Eds.]: Physiology of Emotions. Springfield, Thomas, 1961, pp. 102-103).

part unrelated. Some are messages of information, others of con-
gratulations, etc. There is no central office which picks up all the
messages at each moment and integrates them to any extent at
all. No central office ever has been designed to do so. Yet this
integrative act is precisely what the brain plus its neuron and
muscle connections strives to accomplish. Many are its failures;
many its errors; some of these lead to death, others to lesser forms
of catastrophe. But on the whole, as a rule, the attempt at integration proves a relative success, and on this the survival and
welfare of the individual and even of the race depends.

The success of the response depends upon accurate but selective representation and evaluation of what is important in the
environment as well as upon effective tension-response. We call
this complicated act of man the *universal welfare response*.
While it is too complicated for accurate representation, a suggestive sketch for mnemomic purposes appears in Figure 5 (p. 78).

Chapter VI

PREVIOUS THEORIES OF EMOTION VERSUS THE PRESENT

Several theories of emotion have come to be regarded as classic. More recent views are based chiefly on laboratory animal investigations. After outlining some of these, we can sketch certain common features and certain different features from the holistic view here to be presented. Thereafter we can consider some new principles derived from the present investigations.

Emotion Defined

We can begin with a definition. From what we know today of human as well as of animal reactions, including the present studies, the following definition seems warranted: Emotion is a vegetative-nervous, endocrine response more or less even of the entire nervous system to an event real or imagined, external or internal (see Fig. 5). Neuromuscular activity is increased to apprehend and to meet the event or state of affairs and visceral processes engage in affective evaluation. The emotion is muscularly patterned as in anger, fear, wrath or otherwise to meet the situation as the organism represents and evaluates it through signal codes. Understandably, the patterns change as functions of time. The response may be acute or chronic.

Lange-James Theory

Most noted in the history of psychology has been the Lange-James theory of emotions. This became known at about the turn of the century. Substantially, the authors maintained that previous students were wrong in their conception of time relations. These students had believed that the peripheral phenomena of emotions, such as blushing, fast heartbeat and breathing rate, pal-

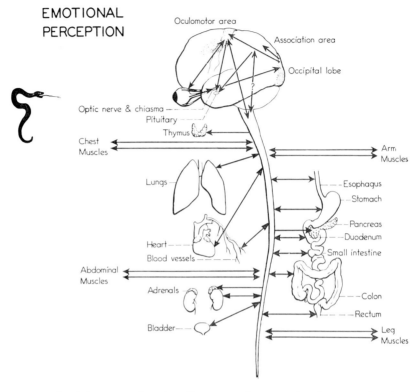

FIGURE 5. Schematic drawing illustrates that emotional perception is a response virtually of the entire organism. Not only are the vegetative nervous system and the organs it supplies aroused but also the skeletal neuromusculature. Accordingly, in emotion we deal with more than a mechanically aroused vegetative nervous response. There is also a complicated network of neuromuscular patterns marking the efforts and the aim of the organism in the emotional state.

pitation, piloerection (in animals), pupillary dilation, weeping, laughing and other familiar phenomena are the expressions or consequences of emotion taking place in the mind or brain. In other words, man has an idea or mental process which takes place centrally in the brain. If it moves him, it is followed by striking expressions in peripheral organs, which tend to adapt him to the stimulus or situation.

Emotion is Belated

This view had largely prevailed until toward the turn of the century, when it was challenged by Lange and by James. They differed from their predecessors in their claim that emotional stimuli arouse peripheral effects before we really experience emotion. They claimed that the emotional experience is a belated affair, for it does not arise until the peripheral phenomena associated with emotion are at least fairly developed. This may require several seconds. We begin to weep, whereupon we feel and sense our weeping, and this feeling and sensing marks when we experience the emotion. Thus, the famous authors claimed that their predecessors had put the cart before the horse.[1] James is credited with ascribing relatively more importance to striated muscle participation, Lange to smooth muscle.

Lange-James Theory Never Proved

The theory of Lange and James helped in their day to bring about a more comprehensive and realistic understanding of the psychophysiology of emotion. Looking backward, we realize that these challengers pointed out the significant role of visceral action, promoting the view that emotional processes do not depend upon the brain alone. As suggested by the lapse of several seconds between the time of stimulus to the emotion and the beginning of the psychogalvanic reflex, they were right that a lag of time often occurs in the development of emotional states. However, the view that visceral action precedes the emotional state and that afferent sensations *thereafter* constitute the subjective phase of the emotion has never been demonstrated in any laboratory.

Nevertheless, it is now possible to discern that the Lange-James theory stood for real progress in the understanding of emotional experience. Assuming, contrary to their view, that in emotion what happens first is perception and thereafter visceral and other peripheral reactions, the fact remains that, once these reactions begin, subjective experience shows that they arouse afferent sen-

---

[1] JAMES, WILLIAM: *The Principles of Psychology*, II. New York, Henry Holt, 1907, Chapter XXV, pp. 442-485.

sations which inevitably constitute part of the developed subjective emotional experience. Thus, though it may be wrong to state that we feel sad because we weep, the emotion experienced inevitably changes upon weeping, due to afferent signals accompanying this act. *In modern terms, we can speak of feedback and reciprocating arousal (or R.A.)* which were unknown in their day. With this drastic modification of their ideology, the Lange-James theory in *certain respects* could stand today.

Physiological evidence against the theory has been said to be the finding that visceral sensations have been shown to be very sparse. This objection reminds one of the familiar anecdote in which the attorney finds his client in jail and upon learning from him the character of the offense objects. "They can't put you in jail for that," whereupon the client replies, "I'm here all the same!" Any experienced observer of subjective phases of emotion can be as confident of the visceral experience in his own emotions as was the client that, despite objections, he was in jail.

A second objection, attributable to G. Marañón, is that, upon administration of adrenalin, producing visceral sensations said to compose emotion, the emotion nevertheless fails to appear unless the appropriate "idea" also is supplied by suggestion or previous experience. James never would have expected otherwise, nor would the present author. A third objection is shared by the present author, namely, that acute emotion sets in more quickly than the visceral changes and does not run parallel with them.

Accordingly, it is safe to assume that, as an emotional state develops in time measured in seconds, afferent sensations play something of the role which Lange and James outlined. However, as will be presented in Chapter VII, we have reason to believe that *the time relations assumed by Lange and James have not been substantiated, and therefore today we can not follow their total ideology.*

Cannon's Theory

In the second and third decades of the century, Walter Cannon approached the matter differently, namely, from the point of view of a physiologist. He was an animal experimentalist rather than an expert in internal observation and performed many well-known studies on cats and dogs during emotional states. Among his discoveries was x-ray visualization and photography of the gastrointestinal tract through the use of bismuth. His extensive studies convinced him that the thalamus is the locus of emotion.[2] The James-Lange theory, he indicates, neglects the thalamic region, which is a coordinating center for emotional reactions. "Processes in the thalamus," he states, "are a source of affective experience." He quotes and agrees with the statement of C. L. Dana: "I am led to the conclusion that emotion is centrally located and results from the action and interaction of the cortex and thalamus."[3] Dana continues: "The centers that control the activities of the vegetative nervous system are mainly in the brain stem. These centers are first appealed to when the animal perceives something calling for instant action in defense, offense, or active desire. They, on the other hand, stir up the muscles, viscera and glands, but they also appeal through the thalamus to the cortex and arouse the emotions appropriate to the object recognized or idea that has been aroused."

Brain Localization

Historical credit must be given to this distinguished physiologist, Walter Cannon, for his success in determining a distinct locality in the brain concerned with emotion. However, as Walshe pointed out, if a particular function is marked by activity in some nerve center and is lost after that nerve center is destroyed, we are warranted in concluding that action of the nerve center participates in the function, but we are not warranted in assuming that the function is "located" in the center.[4]

Accordingly, if it is found that certain emotional states are obliterated or no longer occur if the thalamus is destroyed, we can logically conclude only that the functional integrity of the thalamus is a necessary condition for such emotional states to

[2] CANNON, W. B.: Again the James-Lange and the thalamic theories of emotion. *Psychol. Rev.*, 38:281-295, 1931.

[3] DANA, C. L.: "The Anatomic Seat of the Emotions," *Arch. Neurol. and Psychiat. (Chicago)*, 6:634, 1921.

[4] WALSHE, F. M. R.: On the interpretation of experimental studies of cortical motor function. *Brain*, 47:249, 1951.

occur. The evidence thus secured indicates that thalamic operation occurs in emotion but does not prove that the emotion occurs in the thalamus; in other words, that the thalamus is the "seat" of emotion. As will be recounted in the following chapter, in addition to the thalamus, recent studies implicate subthalamic as well as other limbic lobe regions in the occurrence of emotion, including at least some parts of the neocortex.

Freud's Theory of Emotion

Among theories of emotion most popular today are those of Sigmund Freud. Supported by dream and symptom analysis, these are well known to most neuropsychiatrists. Freud's theory of the emotions, however, does not deal chiefly with the laboratory phenomena considered mostly by Lange, James, Cannon and other physiologists and psychologists but is founded upon concepts largely original with him. For these the reader is referred to his original voluminous writings and to the recent analysis of D. Rapaport.[5] For present purposes and within the limitations of space, we must confine ourselves to a brief, partial sketch.

According to Freud, our emotional life basically depends upon the conflict of two instincts, the life and death-instincts.[6] "Libido is an expression taken from the theory of the emotions. We call by that name . . . the energy of those instincts which have to do with all that may be comprised under the word 'love.'[7] Psychoanalysis . . . gives these love-instincts the name of sexual instincts, a potiori and by reason of their origin."[8] In Freud's terminology, our self-preservative instincts are of a libidinous kind.[6]

However, in the life of the individual as of the race, these tendencies are subject to the laws of development and evolution. Basic patterns of conflict are present in each individual. Their course and resolution differ in each one and depend greatly upon infant sexuality, which is unconscious. Normal development in

[5] RAPAPORT, D.: Emotions and Memory. New York, Int. Univs., 1950.

[6] FREUD, S.: Beyond the Pleasure Principle (Hubback, C. J. M., [Trans.]). New York, Boni & Liveright, p. 67.

[7] FREUD, S.: Group Psychology and the Analysis of the Ego (Strachey, J., [Trans.]). London, Hogarth Press, 1949, p. 37.

[8] Ibid., p. 39.

the early years leads eventually to heterosexuality, but individual differences are common. The development may stop at any stage, if sexual fixation occurs. Furthermore, the general course of character development, according to Freud, can be broadly outlined, for example, in females. Each female develops according to one of three possible courses by which she unconsciously strives to regain the penis which she has lost by castration, also unconsciously.

Freud denies that "psychoanalysis makes sexuality the explanation of everything," for his view is dualistic and he emphasizes the widespread role of "the death instinct" in emotion. An example is sadism, which is "properly a death-instinct." In melancholia, "we find that the excessively strong superego which has obtained a hold upon consciousness rages against the ego with merciless fury, as if it had taken possession of the whole of the sadism available in the person concerned. . . . What is now holding sway is, as it were, a pure culture of the death-instinct."[9]

Freud assumes that what he terms the "ego-instincts" impel us toward death while the sexual instincts impel us toward the preservation of life.[10] He speaks also of the "libidinous instincts of the ego." He distinguishes our conscious from our unconscious life. The greater part of our life, he claims, especially our instinctual desires, is unconscious. The ego extends into a part of our mind which behaves as though it were unconscious; this part Freud names *id* (Es).[11]

"It cannot possibly be disputed," according to Freud, "that the superego, no less than the ego, is derived from auditory impressions; it is part of the ego."[12]

More instinctive than the pleasure principle is the "repetition-compulsion," to which is related not only the play impulse in children and which must be ascribed to the repressed element in the unconscious.[13]

---

[9] Freud, S.: *The Ego and the Id* (Riviere, J., [Trans.]). London, Hogarth Press, 1927, pp. 76-77.

[10] Freud, S.: *Beyond the Pleasure Principle*, pp. 54, 68.

[11] Freud, S.: *The Ego and the Id*, p. 28.

[12] *Ibid.*, p. 76.

[13] Freud, S.: *Beyond the Pleasure Principle*, pp. 24, 19. Repetition-compulsion first put us on the track of the death-instincts (p. 72).

"Anxiety . . . is in the first place something felt."[11] "There are other feelings of unpleasurable character (mental tension, sorrow, grief)."[14] "*Anxiety is the reaction to a situation of danger; and it is circumvented by the ego's doing something to avoid the situation or retreat from it*[14] [italics mine]. "The first anxiety experience, of the human being at least, is birth; and this . . . could be likened to a castration of the mother."[14] "Anxiety in the human being takes the birth process as its prototype."[14] Deprivation of the penis is tantamount to a sexual separation from the mother.[14] "The ego is the real locus of anxiety."[14] "The situation of origin in the case of compulsion neurosis is in fact none other than that in hysteria, namely, the defense necessary against the libidinal demands of the oedipus complex."[14]

"Since it is certainly true that hysteria has a greater affinity with feminity, just as compulsion neurosis has with masculinity, the idea suggests itself that as a determinant of anxiety, loss of love plays a role in hysteria similar to that of the threat of castration in the phobias and dread of the superego in compulsion neurosis."[14]

To what extent each neuropsychiatric reader will follow the views of Freud which lead to emotional theory will depend upon his experience with dream analysis and his predilections. Laboratory evidence to support or invalidate Freud's basic psychophysiological views on emotion has largely been wanting. So far as I know, no one has translated his views into terms which can be thoroughly tested in the laboratory.[15]

From a practical standpoint, we can consider the usefulness thereof. In my personal experience, whatever their usefulness in the treatment of homosexuality, conditions of classic hysteria and one or two other psychoneurotic conditions, I have found the Freudian methods wanting for the successful treatment of anxiety. Analysts who have referred certain cases of anxiety to

---

[14] FREUD, S.: *The Problem of Anxiety* (Bunker, H. A., [Trans.]). New York Psychoanal. Quart. Press and Norton, 1936, pp. 69, 65, 67, 19, 45, 72, 78.

[15] By social and group analysis studies, Trigant Burrow has tried to produce evidence that the libido's dynamic drives and emotions underlie all human conduct. (*The social basis of consciousness—a study in organic psychology*, New York, Harcourt, Brace, 1927).

my clinic would appear to have had to some extent a like experience. A veteran analyst recently trained in physiological methods of tension control reports strikingly improved therapeutic results. These are gained in months where years of analysis failed.

Since the days of Lange, James and Freud, there has been progress toward a more nearly adequate theory of emotions. The progress has been made in three fields, including physiology, psychology and neuropsychiatry, to which we shall proceed in following chapters.

FURTHER COMMENTS ON PREVIOUS THEORIES

Some of the previous theories of emotion apparently were based on a wrong analogy. Unwittingly, it had become traditional among psychologists to assume that the elements of the mind are comparable with the elements discovered in other scientific departments. An example of the latter is the discovery of the basic role of hydrogen, from which all other elements can be compounded.

The would-be discoverers, accordingly, sought one element from which all other mental elements could be compounded. To be sure, they were well aware that mental elements sought were not material, like hydrogen, but in some sense must be "functional" although the term *structural psychology* was in vogue with some of the most conservative experimentalists (e.g., Professor G. E. Müller, E. B. Titchener, etc.). However, this awareness did not deter them from the search.

In consequence, early to be developed was the theory of *mind-dust*, attacked by William James, who in turn sought the primary element (so to call it here) in sensations. Sigmund Freud believed that he had found the elementary instinct, the stuff out of which normality as well as neurosis develops, namely, in the sex instinct, the libido, opposed by the unconscious death wish. Many psychologists have turned to the motor element of elements, developing a "motor theory of consciousness" (sometimes wrongly ascribed to the author) or of emotion (Marston).[16]

---

[16] MARSTON, W. M.: Motor consciousness as a basis for emotion. *Amer. J. Psychol.,* XXII: 140-150, 1927-1928.

Other "primary elements" could be recounted from the history of psychology. Pavlov's conditioned and unconditioned reflex comes close to the same order of search, as one reads that author closely.

The so-called integrative theory of W. M. Marston was in substance that (a) affection is motor consciousness generated by integration of impulses in the sensory centers, and (b) accordingly, all bodily action brought about by activity of the central nervous system is accompanied by affective awareness. We can subscribe to the second assumption while remaining unconvinced by Marston's generalization. A motor theory of emotion, like the motor theory of consciousness (often incorrectly ascribed to the author) neglects many contrary findings.

All such searches for primary elements in psychology, we submit, are initiated on false premises and deserve to become obsolete. A basic chemical has been discovered by chemists, and basic particles are being discovered by physicists. This should not mislead psychologists to prolong their kindred searches.

HOLISTIC ASSUMPTIONS

Instead, the assumption seems opportune that physiological and psychological analyses of emotions and of other behavior and subjective occurrences in man should be supplemented from the standpoint of the engineer. Thus we will take the whole organism into account, namely, the individual person or higher animal. Indeed, like man-made instruments, such as our television sets, our motor cars or our planes, the individual operates as a whole. Emotions and other forms of mental activity are manners of operation of the organism or its parts. From this point of view we are not tempted to try to find a unitary element of elements.

Unlike the particular kinds of man-made instruments mentioned, man and higher animals obviously can be said to be largely self-run. This means that their energy supplies are self-contained and that expenditures of these energies are to an important extent internally regulated.

From the findings of countless investigators, we know that these energy expenditures at any moment depend on and are to some extent mathematical functions of stimuli which appear in the environment, but also internally. Structural mechanisms for the expenditure of these energies along specific directions in response to specific types of stimuli are called instincts. These inbuilt mechanisms have been questioned by certain behaviorists, but are recognized by most biologists. The study of conditioned and unconditioned reflexes introduced by I. Pavlov (if not carried to an extreme) has furnished much of the rationale for understanding how instinctive functions and tendencies can be modified and changed by experience and how a certain educability results.

We can abandon the traditional search of psychologists for a primary element of elements or function of functions without sacrificing the vast knowledge of functions which psychologists and physiologists have achieved. Indeed, we can put this knowledge into better order and appreciate it from a more modern standpoint. We need to synthesize our vast knowledge of details and can do this successfully and less controversially from an engineering standpoint if we recognize that in the sense mentioned above man is an instrument self-run.

This view has been elaborated elsewhere[17] and has been put to practical test. It has proved useful[18] and is readily teachable to relatively young children. Briefly we can summarize here its application to emotions.

In emotional states, the individual is moved to take cognizance, evaluate and to respond to some event, circumstance or condition, real or imagined. Often this is a form of welfare response in which all systems in man take part. The cerebrospinal and striated neuromusculature systems show active patterns insofar as there occurs perception, intellectual evaluation and motor response; in short, there is purposeful effort. The vegetative nervous system, endocrine system and visceral systems, including smooth and cardiac neuromusculature, show coordinate responses, intricately interwoven among each other and also the cerebrospinal responses. *Emotion is distinguished as a more or less or-*

---

[17] JACOBSON, E.: Neuromuscular controls in man: Methods of self-direction in health and in disease. *Amer. J. Psychol.*, 68:549-561, Dec., 1955.

[18] JACOBSON, E.: *Anxiety and Tension Control.* Philadelphia, Lippincott, 1964.

ganized purposive response of the individual to environmental or internal signals and is marked by extraordinary excitation. Indeed, excitation of the vegetative and endocrine systems is the outstanding mark.[19]

In some emotional states, notably, anger and sexual passion, purposively directed attention predominates, and the total patterns lead to accomplishment or deed. In others, disturbance predominates, as in the startle pattern of surprise or in panic. Purposive patterns then are less in evidence and integration if the welfare response is lessened.

In the brain we have evidence for the role of the limbic system (Papez, MacLean).[20] The recent important contribution of S. H. Kraines provides an extended blueprint of the assumed physiological processes of emotion. To be sure, by rounding out and extension, it goes beyond our actual knowledge of today. We can recommend this article and the book of the same author to readers, but in the present volume we shall endeavor to confine ourselves more closely to observations and conclusions.[21]

Before closing this chapter, we quote at length from a scholarly summary on the "localization" of emotion by Lord Brain.[22]

> Thus the more we look for any localized area in the nervous system concerned with emotion, the more it eludes us. From the neurological standpoint any emotional reaction normally involves 1) a state of physiological preparedness, often hormonal; 2) the primary sensory afferent pathways and cortical areas, which furnish the raw material of perception; 3) secondary cortical sensory activity of a discriminative kind leading to recognition of the specific object, which excites emotion, in respect of its position, size, distance, etc., as well as its qualitative

---

[19] In epilepsy in visceral and feverish disease, excitation of both divisions of the nervous system also is in evidence. However, in epileptic attacks, the cerebrospinal system is the more conspicuous. Feverish and visceral disease are easily distinguished from emotional response according to the definitions given.

[20] PAPEZ, J. W.: A proposed mechanism of emotion. *Arch. Neurol (Chicago)*, 38:725, 1937; MacLEAN, P. D.: The limbic system ("visceral brain") and emotional behavior. *Ibid.*, 73:130, 1955.

[21] KRAINES, S. H.: Emotions: A physiologic process. *Psychosomatics, IV* (6): 313-324, Nov.-Dec., 1963.

[22] BRAIN, LORD (ed.): *Recent Advances in Neurology and Neuropsychiatry*. Boston, Little, 7th ed., 1962, p. 44.

nature. 4) There is also a state of heightened perceptual and conative activity leading to 5) the motor response to the object exciting the emotion, e. g. approach, aggression, flight, etc. In addition to the motor response there are 6) other accompanying bodily states, particularly those mediated by the activity of the autonomic nervous system.

It follows from this that we must not expect to find any localized pathway for particular emotions. The individuality of an emotion depends upon a particular combination of the various factors just enumerated. The fact that a single emotion, such as fear, may exceptionally be excited by an epileptic discharge originating in the temporal lobe must not be interpreted as meaning any more than that the discharge in question was capable of arousing the whole complex of physiological activities associated with the emotion of fear. Similarly, there is no evidence in support of the existence of localized pathways for emotion in general viewed as a whole. This, however, does not exclude the existence of localized afferent and efferent (motor and autonomic) pathways concerned in the evocation of emotion and which are localizable. Between them, however, lies a diffuse process concerned with the heightening of the specific activities concerned with each individual emotion.

With certain important modifications, in Chapter VII I shall examine evidence for views related to those quoted above concerning the "localization" of emotion. The evidence to be presented will favor the view that mental activities of every type, including perception, imagination, recollection and attention, are specifically localized only peripherally; that is, they are determined by neuromuscular patterns of the moment.[23] I shall assume that the same is true of behavior patterns.[24] As for brain patterns,

---

[23] FESSARD, A. Le conditionnement considere l'echelle du neurone. *Electroenceph. Clin. Neurophysiol. Mont.*, Suppl. *13*, pp. 157-184, 1960.

[24] "While these investigations have emphasized the involvement of multiple structures within the nervous system in even the simplest sensory associations, they have as yet been unable to associate changes in the electrical activity of the brain with overt behavioral manifestations. Almost no one has asserted that the electroencephalographic changes observed with juxtaposed stimuli bear any direct relation to the behavioral activity of the animal." (WELLS, C. E.: Electroencephalographic correlates of conditioned responses. In GLASER, G. H. [Ed.]: *EEG and Behavior,* New York, Basic Books, 1963, p. 95).

I conclude that we investigators have been on the wrong path since the discovery of the EEG by Hans Berger. We have assumed that we should eventually discover specific EEG patterns in one-to-one correspondence with specific moments of mental activity of behavior. In this search we have failed because we have been expecting to find what really does not exist.

Specification of moments of mental activity and of behavior takes place in peripheral patterns. In most instances, as we shall see, brain patterns for one and (approximately) the same mental or behavioral act are nonspecific. (Exceptions to this rule possibly may be reflexive and sensory neuronal patterns.) In short, we have been "barking up the wrong tree." "Central" can and does make our telephone connections variously in complicated circuits. What become specific are our individual moments of conversation at the periphery of the telephone system. Finally, "central" does not really control or direct what we say. This leads to another question which will be discussed.

Chapter VII

PRESENTING NEW PRINCIPLES OF MIND AND BRAIN

Current Tradition Equivalates Mind and Brain

T HAT mental activity occurs in the brain alone with expressions or consequences elsewhere in the body is the current belief of scientists, generally including physiologists, psychologists and psychiatrists. The "mind" of man and animals is believed to be equivalent to the functional aspects of brain activities. Since this equivalence has usually passed unquestioned, the research of brain physiologists and psychologists today generally is based on the presumptions mentioned. According to the prevalent view, then, imagination, recollection and thinking are performances whose physiological correlates are chiefly in the brain. This view is presented pictorially in Figure 6. A related prevalent view is that "the brain controls behavior."[1]

In the present chapter I shall present the case against these prevalent views. However, in the face of almost universal acceptance, any challenge may seem presumptuous and unreasonable. Without doubt, much *prima facie* evidence has led to the traditional view which makes it all the harder to analyze. History shows that traditions die hard, if at all, especially when partially true.

According to the present argument, the control of mental activity and of behavior has never been experimentally identified and will not be recorded in any portion of the organism because it resides in the integrated totality.[2] That conduct is largely a

---

[1] *Cf.* FESSARD, A. E.: Inf. proc. in the nerv. syst. Vol. III, *Proc. Int. Union Physiol. Sci.* Excerpta Medica Foundation, 1962, p. 417.

[2] The term "control" is often employed by physiologists in the limited sense of the action of one brain region to facilitate or inhibit the action of another; or of

a nerve like the vagus to control the rate of heartbeat; or of the action of hormones on peripheral structures, etc. Titles appearing in the *Proceedings of the 1965 International Congress of Physiological Sciences* include "Cardiovascular Control by the Central Nervous System" (R. F. RUSHMER) and "Control of the Systemic Circulation in Hypoxia" (P. I. KORNER). Further examples can be found in almost any publication in journals of physiology. Thus no objection to this usage is intended or implied. In analogy with engineering terminology, these examples illustrate what are properly termed "automatic controls." They constitute most, if not all, of the subject matter of physiology.

As for total behavior, however, the view here advocated is that it is man himself, the integrated organism, and not merely some part of him, that determines his behavior as a whole. In so doing, his great central communication system, his brain, must function appropriately, but never alone. Even so, it would be misleading to say that he "issues commands" which are carried out in his conduct or that his brain stem issues such commands. There are no commands, for this is but a figurative phrase of unproved tradition, likening man to a nation or an army. Experience shows that man's voluntary behavior is governed by himself. In simple terms which are at the same time accurate, *It is man himself doing!* If we regard physiology as the science of automatic controls within the organism, the important task is to determine the integrated action of tissues and organs, which result in conduct of the whole. However, when physiologists ascribe governmental controls of the whole organism to some part of the brain, they have inadvertently passed beyond the boundaries of physiology and have trespassed into the fields of psychology and psychiatry.

It would be naive to assume that the central or the peripheral nervous system behaves holistically in a literal sense of the word. For competent response to environmental conditions which vary incessantly, appropriate variation is required in the organism, both in vegetative and cerebrospinal departments. Optimum response in man often requires the development of what I have called "differential neuromuscular activity" and "differential relaxation" (*Cf. Prog. Rel.,* U. of Chicago, rev. ed., 1938). What basically corresponds to these differential states in the periphery is currently the subject of investigations by many brain physiologists, under many and divers titles.

→

FIGURE 6. Traditional view. Diagram to illustrate the time order of brain and peripheral phenomena according to the traditional view which is still the current view among doctors and scientists. According to this, brain action precedes neuromuscular and other peripheral action, and the latter is the "expression" of brain ideation or mentation. As shown in the text, this current view of succession is founded on unsupported theory. No laboratory evidence confirms it. It is of course well known that upon stimulation of any cortical cell depolarization effects occur followed by the passage of nerve impulses efferently to a neuromuscular or other peripheral effector. There is no fallacy so far, but fallacy arises when this same order of events is believed to apply to neuromuscular action in the intact organism. Hereupon, with regard to the whole muscle and the brain section involved, the order is approximately simultaneous, not successive.

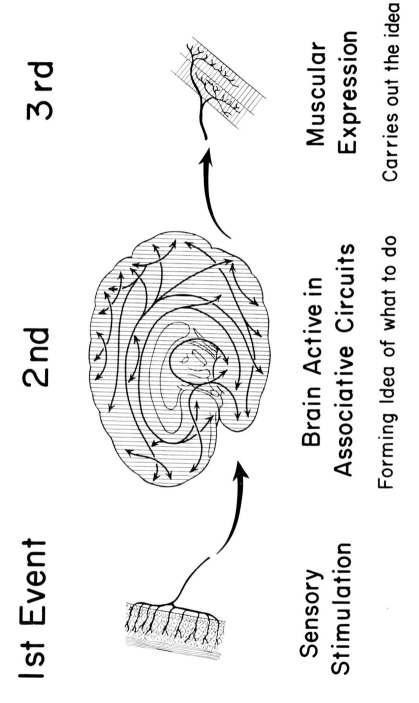

1st Event

2nd

3rd

Sensory
Stimulation

Brain Active in
Associative Circuits

Muscular
Expression

Forming Idea of what to do

Carries out the idea

function of integration rather than the result of action from some locale is beginning to be recognized by some physiologists as is illustrated in the following classic lines freely translated from Henry Gastaut.[3]

> In chronic animal preparations the experiences following stimulation or destruction in the rhinencephalon indicate that this organ is organized for visceral function no less than the neighboring neoencephalon is organized for somatic functioning. These experiences yield manifestations in appearance and conduct which are inextricable from the totality of the individual in what is conventionally called the domain of the vegetative and cerebrospinal systems. From the global, undifferentiated activity of the organism there results conduct related to the satisfaction of needs (search, apprehension and ingestion of foods, rejection of excrements), the perpetuation of the organism, (reproduction) or its defense (emotional behavior with attention, which facilitates the appreciation of danger and prepares the economy for response thereto), from the fear which permits the avoidance of danger by flight from the wrath which permits that the danger be faced in combat.

These lines remind us of the *welfare response,* the term proposed in Chapter I.

Supporting Evidence for the Tradition

That brain tissue activation indispensibly participates in every form of mental operation can be safely assumed. In motor activities, authors refer to the pioneer discoveries of Fritsch and Hitzig and of Ferrier.[4] Modern reviews of brain localization include those of Fulton, of Penfield and Jasper and of Lord Brain.[5] It is

---

[3] GASTAUT, HENRY: Correlations entre le systeme nerveux vegetatif et le systeme de la vie de relation dans le rhinencephale. *J. Physiol., Paris* 44:451-470, 1952.

[4] FRITSCH, G., and HITZIG E.: Über die Elektrische Erregbarkeit des Grosshirns. *Arch. Anat. Physiol.,* 37:300-332, 1870; Ferrier, D.: *The Function of the Brain.* London, Smith Elder, 1876.

[5] FULTON, JOHN: *The Physiology of the Nervous System.* Oxford U. P., 1945, Chapter 20; PENFIELD, W., and JASPER, H.: *Epilepsy and the Functional Anatomy of the Human Brain.* Boston, Little, 1954; BRAIN, LORD. Recent Advances in Neurology and Neuropsychiatry. Boston, Little, 1962.

known that lesions of parts of the brain stem, notably of the centrencephalic system of Penfield, result in unconsciousness. Again, the anencephalic child lies on the floor in a heap, unable to move, think or comprehend. Patients with ascertainable brain pathology suffer defects or changes in their mental functions, which sometimes are corrigible upon surgery. By varying approaches, innumerable investigators have established evidence of mental function to some extent at least apparently associated with specific brain localization. We need not doubt that in some sense and manner prerolandic cortex of man and higher animals is chiefly motor and the postrolandic cortex chiefly sensory. Recently, much information has resulted upon electrical stimulation of electrodes implanted in human as well as animal brains.[6] The literature on motor, sensory and other brain localization is too vast to be here reviewed, nor is this necessary.

In a forthcoming volume I shall review electroencephalic observations and the attempt to correlate them with the occurrence of mental activities.[7] While this has often proved successful to a limited extent, the results on the whole up to date have proved disappointing. This includes our own electroencephalographic studies, which will be briefly mentioned later in this chapter.

Clearly, then, our present thesis will assume that some form of brain action is required in every moment of mental activity. Thus the evidence that brain action is necessary for mental activity will not be denied. However, there will remain an open question: Is it sufficient? I shall favor a negative answer.

The present studies had shown that "there are no closed circuits in the brain," according to Ralph Lillie in 1934. Our results over the years confirm the view that *in mental activities of all forms there are no closed physiological circuits in the brain. Our evidence suggests that at the moment of occurrence of any form of mental activity, the physiological circuits include not only associative, afferent and efferent brain neurones, axons and dendrites, but also afferent and efferent nerve activities and*

---

[6] HEATH, R. G.: Electrical self-stimulation of the brain in man. *Amer. J. Psychiat.*, 120 (6):571-574, Dec., 1963; *The Role of pleasure in Behavior.* New York, Harper, 1964.
[7] JACOBSON, E.: *Physiological Psychiatry,* 1968.

peripheral activities chiefly in the form of muscle contraction. The contraction turns out to be specifically patterned in each such moment.

Evidence for Present Thesis

There is evidence for the present thesis including the following:

1. Our trained observers of sensory, emotional and other internal experiences, including myself, uniformly report specific image-neuromuscular signal patterns subjectively appearing at the instant of acts properly termed *mental*. To the trained observer, these signal patterns are one and the same as the mental activities. Thus, to the subject, the time relations are ipso facto identical. These acts include imagination, recollection, perception and emotion. Indeed they include any and every mental act of types of interest to the psychologist or practical importance to the neuropsychiatrist.[8] Scientific standards require that observers' reports be carefully controlled. Only investigators long experienced in autosensory observation are sufficiently prepared to do this critically. Unfortunately, courses of instruction in autosensory observation have not yet become standard in uni-

---

[8] JACOBSON, E.: Experiments on the inhibition of sensations. *Psychol. Rev.,* *18*:24-53, (Jan.), 1911; Further experiments on the inhibition of sensations. *Amer. J. Psychol.,* 23:345-369, (July), 1912; On meaning and understanding. *Ibid* 22:553-577, (Oct.) 1911; The use of experimental psychology in the practice of medicine. *JAMA,* 77:342-347, (July 30), 1921; The technic of progressive relaxation. *J. Nerv. Ment. Dis.,* 60 (6):568-578, (Dec.) 1924; Progressive relaxation. *Amer. J. Psychol.,* 36:73-87, Jan. 1925. Also see the following references. Electrical Measurements of Neuromuscular States During Mental Activities: a. Imagination of movement involving skeletal muscle. *Amer. J. Physiol.,* *91*(2): 567-608, Jan., 1930; b. Imagination and recollection of various muscular acts. *Amer. J. Physiol.,* 94(1):22-34, July, 1930; c. Visual imagination and recollection. *Amer. J. Physiol.,* 95(3):694-702, Dec., 1930; d. Evidence of contraction of specific muscles during imagination. *Amer. J. Physiol.,* 95(3)703-712, Dec., 1930; e. Variation of specific muscles contracting during imagination. *Amer. J. Physiol.,* 96(1):115-121, Jan. 1931; f. A note on mental activities concerning an amputated limb. *Amer. J. Physiol.,* 96(1):122-125, Jan., 1931; g. Imagination, recollection and abstract thinking, involving the speech musculature. *Amer. J. Physiol.,* 97(1):200-209, April, 1931. Electrophysiology of mental activities. *Amer. J. Psychol.,* 44:677-694, Oct., 1932; Measurement of action-potentials in the peripheral nerves of man without anesthetic. *Proc. Soc. Exp. Biol. Med.,* 30:713-715, 1933; Electrical measurement of activities in nerve and muscle. In: Bentley, M., *et al.* (ed.). *The Problem of Mental Disorder.* N. Y. McGraw-Hill, 1934, pp. 133-145.

versity curricula. Often, psychologists lacking this essential training nevertheless publish "authoritative" conclusions on mental
activity. They can be likened to "authorities" on chemistry who
have seldom or never received laboratory training.

Mental Activities of All Types Include Neuromuscular
Patterns Which Are Specific

2. Objective electrophysiological identification, measurement
and photographic recording of neuromuscular tension patterns
have been repeatedly reported from this laboratory: from 1927 to
1936, in the Physiological Department of the University of Chicago, and since 1936, in the Laboratory for Clinical Physiology.
These recordings have been made almost daily. Thus, they provide a uniquely vast series of records, much more extensive than
those commonly obtained in most laboratory investigations, whatever the field of science.[8] Many of these findings have been confirmed in other laboratories, within the limits of their electronic
equipment.[9]

---

[8] Max, L. W.: An experimental study of the motor theory of consciousness. 2.
Method and apparatus. *J. Gen. Psychol.* 13:153-175, 1935; 3. Action-current responses in deaf mutes during sleep, sensory stimulation and dreams. *J. Comp.
Psychol.,* 19:469-486, 1935; 4. Action-current responses in the deaf during awaken-
ing, kinesthetic imagery and abstract thinking. *Ibid.,* 24:301-344, 1937; Clites
Myron S.: Somatic activities in relation to successful and unsuccessful problem
solving. Part 3. Action potentials and muscular movements and tensions; *J. Exp.
Psychol.,* 19: 172-192, 1936; Freeman, G. L.: Changes in tonus during completed
and interrupted mental work., *J. Gen. Psychol.,* 4:309-334, 1930; Spread of neuromuscular activity during mental work. *Ibid.,* 5:479-494, 1931; Facilitative and inhibitory effects of muscular tension upon performance. *Amer. J. Psychol.,* 45:17-52,
1933; Shaw, William A.: The distribution of muscular action potentials during
imaging. *Psychol. Rec.* 2:195-216, 1938; Relation of muscular action potentials to
imaginal weight lifting. *Arch. Psychol.,* 35 (247), Feb., 1940; Davis, R. C.: Patterns
of muscular activity during 'mental' work and their constancy. *J. Exp. Psychol.,*
24:451-465, 1939; Gould, Louis N.: Verbal hallucinations and activity of vocal
musculature. An electromyographic study. *Amer. J. Psychiat.,* 105:367-372, Nov.,
1948; Auditory hallucinations and subvocal speech. *J. Nerv. Ment. Dis.,* 190:418-427,
1949; Dement, W., and Kleitman, M.: The relation of eye movements during sleep
to dream activity. An objective method for the study of dreaming., *J., Exp. Psychol.,*
53:339-346, May, 1957; Whatmore, George B., and Ellis, Richard M., Jr.; Some
neurophysiologic aspects of depressed states. *Arch. Gen. Psychiat. (Chicago),* 1:70-80,
July, 1959; Some motor aspects of schizophrenia: An EMG study. *Amer. J. Psychiat.,*
114:882-889, April, 1958.

*Mental Activities Diminish to Vanishing Point With the
Neuromuscular Patterns*

3. In hundreds of individuals highly trained and skilled in
autosensory observation and in neuromuscular relaxation, as
measured at the instant of the experimental test, we have found
uniformly that when action-potential values, especially of the
eye and speech musculature, are in the neighborhood of zero
levels (under one microvolt), the individual reports coordinate
diminution or disappearance of his perceptual, memory, emotional and other mental activity. To those who are unfamiliar
with this phenomenon, it is important to clarify that the subject's
task is only to relax muscles; he is not instructed or informed
what to expect in regard to mental operations upon extreme
relaxation. The degree of relaxation is determined simultaneously
on the specialized, sensitive neurovoltmeters employed. Psychological tests readily show that the subject is neither in a suggesti-
ble state nor in any degree or form of a trance state. Often we
have employed highly skeptical individuals with the same ultimate findings, once they have become experienced, careful observers.

Vacuous Facies

4. The individual who relaxes under controlled conditions to
near-zero levels manifests an expressionless facies. Those wit-
nessing the appearance agree that he appears strikingly free from
emotion, and even from perception or reflection. Thus, the absence of mental activity is indicated by *prima facie* evidence
even to the uninitiated. The eyes, if open, do not look. The
appearance is not like that of any hypnoidal or hypnotic state.
The knee jerk is diminished or absent instead of being lively,
as commonly in hypnosis. There is no *rapport*, no increased sug-
gestibility, no need to awaken the individual by any word or
form of suggestion or other type of instruction.

From extensive observations under controlled conditions over
decades of laboratory and clinical investigation, I feel warranted
in generalizing that *every mental act of perception, imagination,
fantasy, recollection, reflection or emotion at the moment of oc-*

currence is a function measurable and recordable in neuromuscular action potential patterns no less than a function of brain-spinal cord patterns.

Time Relations

5. Presently we are studying the time relations of muscular acts and brain activities. The traditional view implies that our muscular acts express what the brain determines. It assumes that our muscular acts are controlled by the brain. Since the days of Fritsch and Hitzig it has been known that electrical and other stimulation of cortical motor centers incites peripheral muscular activities. Without doubt, under such stimulation, brain control of certain movements actually is evidenced. I do not question this. However, the conditions of stimulation mentioned are artificial and exist as a rule only in the laboratory. Under daily conditions of natural animal life, direct electrical stimulation of the brain does not occur. The question remains whether similar relations between brain and muscle activity characterize normal behavior of the intact person or animal? We can ask whether brain action characteristically precedes and programs muscular conduct as a rule in the normal behavior of intact man and animal?

When the brain is stimulated electrically, no doubt exists but that the brain action begins first and conditions the peripheral action. However, the time relations evidently are reversed when sense organs in the skin, muscle or other peripheral structure are the site of effective stimulation. Obviously, the physiological response then begins peripherally rather than centrally. Thus, no one should assert that in sensation and perception brain action always is initiated before peripheral actions. Even so, the question remains: What are the time relations in "voluntary" acts of intact man, namely, those involving the skeletal musculature?

Pertinent Recordings by Other Investigators

Before presenting our own recordings we shall examine records published by others which bear upon time relations of brain and periphery in mental activities, although the authors did not have

PRECENTRAL HAND

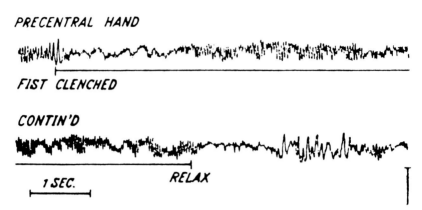

FIST CLENCHED

CONTIN'D

1 SEC.   RELAX

FIGURE 7. Electrocorticogram from the precentral hand area of the left hemisphere during clenching of the right fist. Note the arrest of beta rhythm at the beginning and at the end of the sustained contraction, but not during the maintenance of a continuous contraction. (From Jasper and Penfield, 1949, our reference—[see present text].)

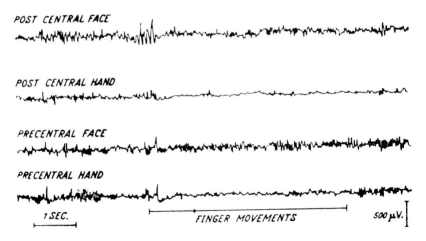

POST CENTRAL FACE

POST CENTRAL HAND

PRECENTRAL FACE

PRECENTRAL HAND

1 SEC.   FINGER MOVEMENTS   500 μV.

FIGURE 8. Electrocorticograms taken simultaneously from the post central face and hand areas and from the precentral face and hand areas during continuing movements of the fingers (successive touching of fingers to the thumb). (From Jasper and Penfield, 1949, our reference [see present text].)

it under consideration. Prerequisite is simultaneous recording of peripheral and central electrical phenomena with clear indication of time relations. I have found very few of this precise nature. However, Figure 7 is taken from a recording of Jasper and Penfield.[10] The precentral beta rhythm which they recorded shows arrest in connection with the onset of clenching of the fist. As indicated by the signal time-line, if the traditional theory of muscle group control by the brain is justified, the onset of this change in brain rhythm ought to precede the flexor muscular activity of fist clenching, but it does not. Instead, the onset of muscular contraction precedes that of beta rhythm change. Furthermore, upon the signal to relax, the change in beta brain rhythm *follows* the muscular phenomenon. Another recording by the same investigators is shown in Figure 8. Successive continuous movements of the fingers, such as touching the thumb to each finger in rapid succession, was attended by a continuous diminution of the beta rhythm recorded from the precentral gyrus, which is predominantly motor. Simultaneously (I note) there was diminution of electrical activity of the post central hand area and to some extent that of the post central face regions.

J. A. V. Bates wrote an important article entitled "Electrical Activity of the Cortex Accompanying Movement."[11] He found no evidence justifying the belief that preceding the onset of a voluntary movement in man there is some activity of the large pyramidal (Betz cells) in the precentral gyrus. This failure agreed with foregoing results of others. Regarding his recordings through the skull from electrodes situated over the vicinity of the hand muscle region of the motor cortex, he states, ". . . on no occasion has there been any activity recorded preceding the onset of the movement. The most usual response was one in which the eletrode over the region of the central sulcus became negative with respect to the rest of the brain, and this effect began 20 to 35 milliseconds after the muscle activity reaching a peak in 55 to 75 milliseconds and lasting for 100 to 200 milli-

---

[10] JASPER, H., and PENFIELD, W.: Zur Deutung des normalen Elektrencephalo-gramms and seiner Veränderungen. *Arch. Psychiat. v. Ztschr. Neurol., 183*:169, 1949.
[11] *J. Physiol., 113*:240-257, 1951.

seconds (p. 246)." He found no evidence of any slow (dc) potential EEG swing preceding the onset of EMG (p. 248). Special tests led him to conclude that the EEG recordings resulted from proprioceptive impulses from the muscle regions.

In all of the foregoing instances, the onset of the brain wave changes apparently follows the onset of the muscular contraction. This, again, is contrary to what we should expect under the traditional theory according to which the brain, so to speak, gives out "central commands" to muscles.[12]

What I question is whether in mental operations brain action precedes muscular patterns sufficiently to program them as is commonly believed.[13]

Instead, the findings of Jasper and Penfield harmonize with my interpretation that, in the muscular acts which they studied, the effective neuronic pathways pass through brain and muscle

---

[12] These words appear in PAILLARD, JACQUES: The patterning of skilled movements. In *Handbook of Physiology Neurophysiology*, III. Amer. Physiol. Soc., 1960, Chapter LXVII, p. 1703.

[13] H. Caspers studied the relations of steady potential shifts in the cortex to the wakefulness-sleep spectrum (in BRAZIER, M.A.B. (Ed.): *Brain Function*. Berkeley, U. Calif., 1963, pp. 177-213). His subjects were freely moving rats with chronically implanted brain electrodes. "In the awake, freely moving animal the steady (D.C. component) of the cerebral cortex exhibits considerable fluctuations," he states, "most of which are strictly synchronized with behavioral activity changes" (p. 178). Upon recording from motor fields, there are "irregular negative waves which correspond to the initiation of each single motor action. In these cases, the first visible displacement of the surface steady potential often precedes the detectable changes in peripheral activity of the animal." He does not state by how much. In the records appearing in his communication, with one exception, we fail to find evidence of any precedence in the case of motor activities. Instead, the time of onset, if anything, appears simultaneous. Precedence of onset of displacement of steady potential characterizes not the motor but the sensory recordings.

Recently, likewise, J. L. O'Leary has presented an investigation entitled "The Direct Cortical Response" (MINGRINO, S., COXE, W. S., KATZ, R. and GOLDRING, S.: In Moruzzi, G., Fessard, A., and Jasper, H. H. [Eds.]: *Progress in Brain Research*, Vol. 1, *Brain Mechanisms*. New York, Amer. Elsevier, 1963, pp. 241-257).

The authors refer to Adrian's (1936) findings of d.c. cortical response following repetitive electrical shocks of weak intensity. "Change to positive polarity signified the activity of pyramidal cells in the cortical depth. . . ." This change "was a necessary prelude to the development of either muscle contraction or cortical afterdischarge." Observations of the author differ in several respects from those of Adrian but will not be discussed here since we do not question the response of muscles to electrical stimulation of the motor cortex.

circuits with continuing reciprocal impulses back and forth, motor and sensory, between brain and muscle upon the initiation, during and at or toward the end of the acts.

Reciprocating Action

If this is true, it would seem to deserve special terminology. I suggest that we might call this neurophysiological action of brain-peripheral circuits the reciprocating activation (R.A.) between brain and neuromuscular and other peripheral effector and hence affective pathways. "R.A.," I believe, is of basic importance in neuro-muscular physiology. The new term suggested would seem to apply here better than would the term *feedback*. Our evidence leads us to recognize that *mental operations are constituted by reciprocal retroactivating brain-neuromuscular patterns*.

The Power Factor

The power factor in "information processing" has received little attention. At the 1962 meeting of scientists in Leyden on information processing of the nervous system this was largely neglected.[14] In consequence, brain physiology was presented as if equivalent to *black box* action, namely, as if brain action occurs without a power factor.

According to the present interpretation, the power factor is present in intact man or animal by virtue of R.A. circuit action. The power factor, we assume, is not the consequence of brain action but is part of the entire operating circuit, which in mental activity apparently includes not only brain, but also cord, peripheral nerves and specifically muscles.

Physiological Circuits

In the words of A. J. Carlson, my investigations have shown that mental activities are muscular acts. I wish to emphasize that these acts are often miniscule. However, in employing the term *circuit*, no strict analogy is intended with the use of this term in

---

[14] *Proceedings of the International Union of Physiological Sciences.* Excerpta Medica Foundation, 1962.

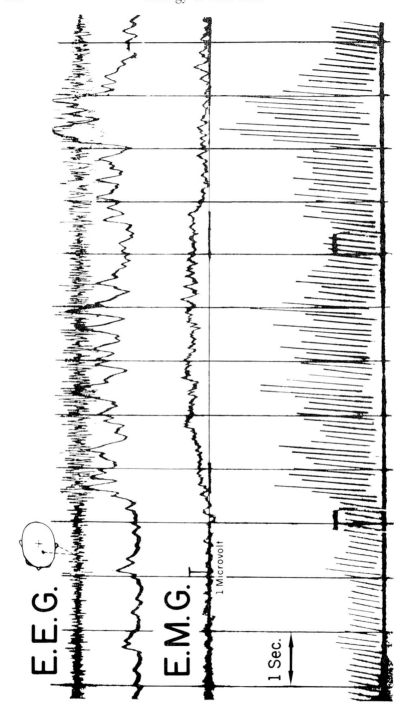

electronics. It seems justified and useful to speak of physiological circuits, which may include synaptic as well as sense-organ connections.

In the foregoing interpretations of time relations of the recordings reproduced in Figures 7 and 8, I have assumed that the signal lines indicating "fist clenched" and "finger movements" were electrically recorded and therefore were accurately timed. However, the authors did not state how these signal lines were recorded. We now proceed to our own recordings, where both brain and muscular recordings are direct photographs from oscillographic light beams. Here the recording beam is weightless and we can be certain of precise time relations.

Our Simultaneous Recordings

Figure 9 presents a recording of this precise type. The signal line which is indicated by an arrow marks the electrically re-

←

FIGURE 9. The beginning of the first break in the signal line at the bottom of the record marks a circuit break in a capacitor discharge through a loud speaker. The click signifies to the subject that he is to clench his right fingers promptly. Upon the second click he is to relax promptly.

Simultaneous monopolar EEG from left frontal region in man (a) 15-20 cps and (b) integrated plus (c) integrated EMG from right hand flexor muscles in man. Lowermost tracing shows integrated EEG at 0.1 second intervals. Read from top to bottom and from left to right. Time periods of all curves are accurate, since weightless oscillographic light beam motions are directly photographed.

The uppermost curve, EEG traces waves over a range of 15-20 cps with little overlap above and below. The different electrode was placed on the scalp over the (estimated) prerolandic "motor center" of the right hand flexor muscles while the indifferent electrode was on the left earlobe.

Comparing onset times, the EMG increase marking righthand flexor muscle contraction occurs at the same instant as the action potential increase shown in the three EEG tracings. The reaction-time is 0.5 second (counting from the beginning of the recorded signal to clench the fingers). Comparing duration and termination times, the muscle potentials occur simultaneously with EEG increased potentials for 4.4 seconds but outlast the EEG increase for about 1.0 second, 0.7 second before the action-potentials from right finger flexion terminates, brain potential increase recurs, outlasting the EMG increase by 2.4 seconds (not shown in record). (The significance of this recurrence is perplexing. The rate of the record per second would need to be faster to permit precise determination of instants of onset.)

corded timing of a click which by previous agreement with the subject is to be the signal for him to squeeze a ball lying in his hand. (Accordingly, this signal or an analogous one does not appear and has no counterpart in the figures of Jasper and Penfield.)

At the top of Figure 9 is a photographic monopolar recording of an oscillographic tracing from the left frontal region in man accurately filtered to include the range of 15 to 20 cps with a little overlap. The second tracing is from the same leads and filters, but has been passed through a bridge rectifier, with a capacitor across the bridge output. After rectification, the action-potentials are thus integrated. Accordingly, thereby we secure a clearer indication of the onset of increase of amplitude of brain waves than would be available from the uppermost tracing alone.

The third tracing is a photographic recording of bipolar os-cillographic beam movement from electrodes on flexor muscles of the right hand before, during and after squeezing the ball. This is an integrated curve made with the integrating neurovolt-meter.[15] The onset of contraction appears approximately at the same instant as the onset of increased amplitude of the brain waves.

Thus there is no evidence here of brain activity preceding the muscular pattern as the traditional theory requires. On the con-trary, the onset of both is approximately simultaneous. This can be interpreted harmoniously with the assumption that brain circuits are not closed within that organ but are continued and completed through muscle.

The fourth tracing can be regarded as confirming what has been said above regarding the second tracing. In the fourth trac-ing the same voltage as appears on the second tracing has charged a large capacitor which is discharged at intervals of 0.1 second by a relay. Thus the vertical lines represent the magnitude of voltage charge over 0.1 second intervals. Accordingly, the time of onset is somewhat less accurately indicated than in Curve 2.

---

[15] JACOBSON, E.: An integrating voltmeter for the study of nerve and muscle potentials, *Rev. Scient. Instrum.* 11 (12):415-418, Dec., 1940.

but the amount of increased voltage per 0.1 second period is more clearly delineated. There is agreement between the data presented by Curves 2 and 4.

Traditional Theory Not Confirmed

In general, the time relations afford no confirmation of the classic traditional theory that brain action controls muscle group action in voluntary activities. On the contrary, these results are interpreted as indicating that brain and muscle action in voluntary activities are interlaced and thus are not separable in time. Briefly restated, this record illustrates that in mental operations there is little or no evidence that circuits are closed in the brain but that instead they are continuously extended in and through muscles.

Along the same lines, Figure 10 presents direct photographs of oscillographic tracings from the right frontal and from the right occipital regions. One right frontal electrode is placed over the presumed "motor center" of the left hand muscles of the prerolandic cortex. The other electrode is placed on the right earlobe to yield a monopolar recording. Likewise, the occipital electrodes are set for monopolar recordings.

Following soon after the signal to the subject to clench his left fingers, the first to appear on our recordings are increased microvoltages not from brain waves of motor and occipital centers but from peripheral potentials.

Incidentally, the increase lasts about 0.1 second, being followed by a decrease to resting values, lasting about 0.07 second. At 1.2 second after the beginning of the signal mark, moderate increase is resumed. The recording from flexor muscles shows a peak value of 8 microvolts, which is about ten times the control value prior to the signal.

This is the recorded temporal onset of flexor muscle potential increase, and it precedes the onset of frontal and occipital EEG increase by about 0.1 second.

Extensor muscle potentials, representing the contraction of antagonists, are recorded. Their time relations are of lesser importance. Their physiologic importance for us lies chiefly in the fact that 330 milliseconds after the recorded beginning of the

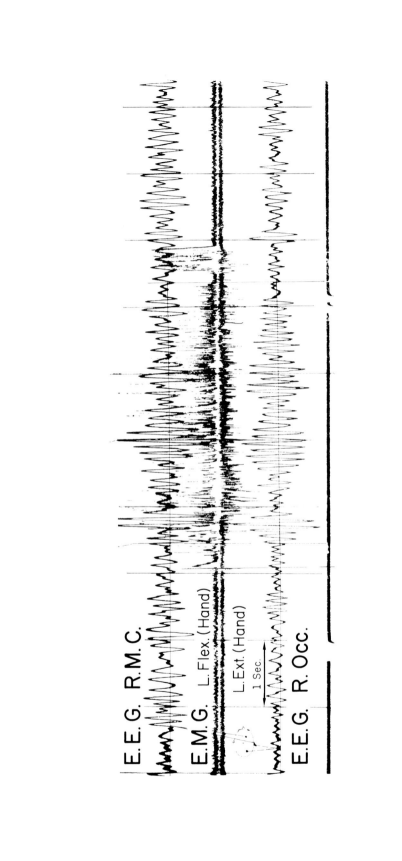

E.E.G. R.M.C.

E.M.G. L. Flex. (Hand)

L. Ext. (Hand)

1 Sec.

E.E.G. R. Occ.

signal to relax the finger muscles, they do relax to values of the same order as prevailed before the signal to clench the fingers; i.e., they return to prior control, i.e., resting values. The indicated relaxation of flexor and extensor muscles lasts about 0.1 second, whereupon there occurs a spurt of flexor and extensor muscle microvoltages respectively lasting 0.3 second and 0.27 second, with peak microvoltages above fifteen microvolts and thirteen microvolts. In this spurt, however, most of the highest spikes from flexor muscles considerably exceed those from extensors.

In subjects trained to relax, such spurts are characteristically absent. However, this subject was not so trained. Accordingly, we interpret this spurt as failure to relax on the first attempt but the record shows successful persistent muscular relaxation following this spurt.

←

FIGURE 10. As for Figure 9, with the first break in the signal line at the bottom of the record, the subject hears a click, which is the signal for him to clench the fingers of his left hand. Upon the second signal, he is to relax these fingers.

Simultaneous monopolar EEGs from the right frontal and right occipital regions are shown respectively in the uppermost and lower-tracing (just above the signal line). The different electrode was placed over the estimated left hand "motor center" of the prerolandic cortex. These tracings cover the frequency range 6 to 15, with a little overlap above and below. The EMG tracings are made with the neurovoltmeter, but are half-wave rectifications. (If the waves were unrectified they would be of twice the amplitude but would have a midpoint at the isoelectric line.)

EMG bipolar action-potential recordings from left hand flexor muscles appear in the median portion of the record just above those from the extensor muscles. Ultrasensitive and ultrastable equipment is employed. Evidently as would be expected during clenching, flexor muscles are more vigorously contracted than extensors.

One second after the beginning of the recorded signal upon which the subject is to clench the left fingers, flexor muscle action potentials increase, indicating the onset of clenching. As yet, no increase of recorded frontal or occipital EEG waves has begun.

The extensor muscle potentials which mark the left fingers precede the increase of the frontal and occipital EEG increase by 0.1 second and continues for 0.2 second following the cessation of the EEG increase. Otherwise the brain and muscle potentials occur simultaneously.

It is possible to check the brain tracings with the integraph so as to secure area values which doubtless indicate total voltage values (charge) over time. Thus checked, we find that the occipital recording gives a value of 300 per cent of control values taken as 100 per cent. The prerolandic recording gives a value of 150 per cent. The significance, if any, of the findings mentioned in this paragraph can not be considered here.

Brain and Muscle Operate Simultaneously in One Nexus

All in all, Figure 10, like Figure 9, supports the conclusion that brain and muscle operate simultaneously in one complicated nexus during mental activity. Central nervous regions do not prevail over an allegedly subordinate peripheral region.

In no sense does this demote brain action. Rather, it enables us in a general way truly to understand the significant role of the brain without ascribing to it functions which it performs in part but by no means exclusively. It might be naïve to say that "we think with our muscles" but it would be inaccurate to say that we think without them.

I desired to repeat the observations of Jasper and Penfield on clenching of the fist with recordings from the prerolandic region. Their great advantage was the opportunity to place electrodes over the brain bared in connection with surgery. Lacking this opportunity in man, I resorted to the classic but less exact method of Krönlein for locating the fissure of Rolando. (This procedure was employed also for recordings illustrated in Figs. 9 and 10.)[16] For present purposes of investigating time relations between central and peripheral events, I have added the use of the integrating neurovoltmeter, which uniquely yields readings to a small fraction of a transient microvolt.

In Figure 11 are tracings in man (respectively from top to bottom) (a) of monopolar EEG from the vicinity of right hand "center" in left "motor cortex" filtered to over the range of 10 to 20 cps with a little overlap above and below; (b) bipolar EMG

---

[16] We have used cats with electrodes implanted in the front paw region of the prerolandic cortex by sterotaxic methods. The test of success is movement of the paw elicited by light electrical stimulation.

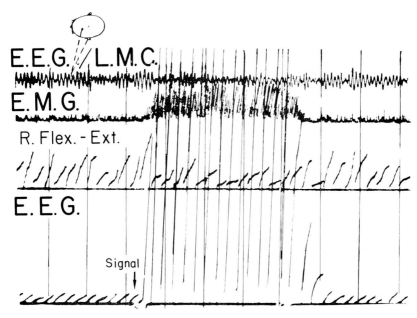

FIGURE 11. Uppermost is monopolar EEG tracing in man from the presumed vicinity of the right hand motor center in the left prerolandic cortex filtered to cover the range of 10 to 20 cps with a little overlap above and below. (b) Below (a) is bipolar EMG from right forearm muscles which flex and extend the fingers; (c) Below (b) is tracing showing integrated values of EEG, produced at intervals of 0.25 per second by discharge of a condenser on which action-potential charge has accumulated; (d) Below (c) is tracing showing integrated values of the EMG similarly and sychronously produced. As will be seen, action-potentials indicating contraction of muscles which act to clench the fist begin and end approximately simultaneously with diminution of EEG voltages. This contrasts with augmentation of EEG voltages shown in our Figures 9 and 10.

from arm muscles which flex and which extend the fingers; (c) integrated values of EEG, produced at intervals of 0.25 per second by discharge of a condenser on which action-potential charge has accumulated; (d) integrated values of the EMG similarly and synchronously produced.

Accordingly, the integrated values of EEG and EMG can be compared for precisely the same interval, namely, 0.25 second.

In this recording the duration of action-potential from muscles

which clench the fist is approximately simultaneous with diminution of the EEG voltages. This contrasts with the augmentation
of EEG voltages shown in our Figures 9 and 10.

The onset of EEG diminution follows the onset of EMG increase by about 0.25 second. Finally the EMG increase outlasts
the EEG diminution by 0.45 second. (Diminution of EEG recurs
0.19 second after the termination of the EMG increase, lasting
0.32 second).

Like Jasper and Penfield and like Gastaut,[17] Sem-Jacobsen,
et al. record diminution of EEG from the motor area during
muscular activity. However, the latter employ depth recording.[18]
From certain of the foregoing studies, J. Paillard concludes that
"a blocking of the rolandic beta rhythm appears where a voluntary movement is being initiated and persists during its execution."[19]

With Voluntary Movements Voltage May Decrease or Increase

"We have never observed an increase in voltage of activity
from the precentral gyrus during voluntary movements," state
Jasper and Penfield.[20] However, according to our own frequent
findings, this is true sometimes *but by no means always.* In many
of our recordings during voluntary movements, the EEG (from
the vicinity of the corresponding "center" of the prerolandic cortex) is increased. Sometimes there is "blocking" but often the
opposite appears.

Our results and conclusions differ in a second important respect
from those of Jasper and Penfield. They observe that the precentral beta rhythm (which they consider characteristic of the "resting" motor cortex in a manner analogous to the alpha rhythm for
the occipital cortex) is *not* sustained (contrary to Paillard) during

---

[17] GASTAUT, H.: *Rev. Neurol.,* 87:176, 1952; *J. Physiol. (Paris),* 44:431, 1952.

[18] SEM-JACOBSEN, C. W. PETERSON, M. C., DODGE, H. W., JR., LAZARTE, J. A., and
HOLMAN, C. B.: Electroencephalographic rhythms from the depths of the parietal,
occipital and temporal lobes in man. *Electroenceph. Clin. Neurophysiol.,* 8:263-278,
May, 1956.

[19] PAILLARD, J.: The patterning of skilled movements. *Neurophysiology,* III. Amer.
Physiol. Soc., 1960, Chapter LXVII, p. 1696.

[20] JASPER and PENFIELD, *loc. cit.,* p. 171.

a maintained contraction, such as clenching the fist, but blocking occurs at the beginning and cessation of an act.[21] In other words, these investigators find the same kind of EEG response for muscular tension as for relaxation.

Relaxation Requires EMG Confirmation

According to my experience, however, individuals often do not relax upon request but, instead, they contract again in an *effort to relax*. This experience is based upon repeated neuromuscular potential recordings. To be sure that they *really relax*, the EMG must be taken. In the studies mentioned, the authors did not do this. In our studies, generally made with healthy individuals trained to relax, the relaxation of the muscles flexing the hand was demonstrated by neuromuscular recordings. If contraction blocked the EEG potentials, as in Figure 11, relaxation returned them to the resting values. In those instances where contraction increased the EEG, as in Figures 9 and 10, relaxation diminished them to resting levels.

Recordings from Laboratory Animals

To overcome the disadvantage permanently of leading through the skull, we employed unanesthetized laboratory animals (cats) with nichrome coil electrodes embedded in the prerolandic area, in or near the "center" for movement of the front or hind paw. The location of the electrodes was confirmed upon movement of the paw upon stimulation with biphasic square wave voltage of about 8 to 12.

In Figure 12, the upper two tracings are EEG photographic recordings from oscillographic light-beam movements, employing direct current amplification. Electrodes are in the right prerolandic hind-paw region. The frequency range covered is zero to fifteen, with a little overlap on the upper side. Each cat was in a cage but otherwise without restraint. Movements were spontaneous without any form of electrical, mechanical or other stimulation.

---

[21] JASPER and PENFIELD, loc. cit., pp. 171, 173.

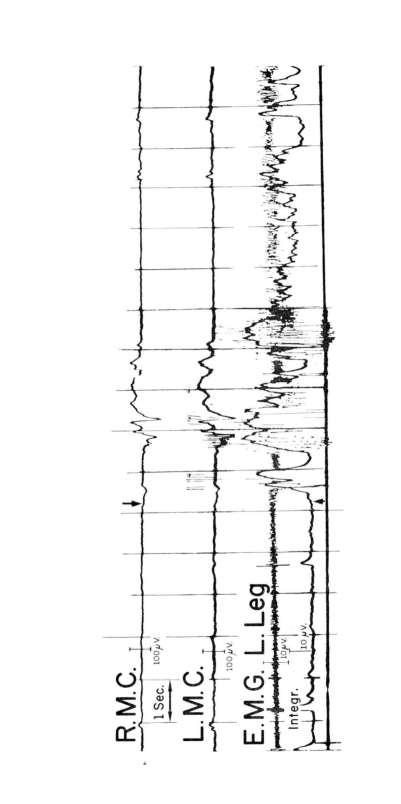

The lower two tracings are bipolar EMG from platinum iridium needle electrodes (both) in the leg extensor muscles in the left thigh. Of these the upper tracing (third from the top) represents a frequency range on the order of 50 to 500 cps. The lowermost tracing is made with the neurovoltmeter, registering the muscle potentials averaged at each instant.

As will be seen, the onset of electrically indicated left hind-paw muscular contraction shows a vigorous onset on the order of seventeen microvolts at the same moment as the onset of seventeen microvolts positive change from the right prerolandic EEG. Thereafter this EEG curve quickly returns negatively, but then for about 1.4 second gradually changes positively to the seventeen microvolt order. During this positive change, the muscle voltages continue high, except during an interval of 0.4 second, when they resume resting values. Following this, the muscle potentials abruptly increase to peak twenty-six microvolt values. Simultaneously there is slight further positive right EEG change followed by full swing positive and negative (EEG) waves, peaking 160 microvolts. Resting right EEG values return after about three second of such waves. During these waves, however, the EMG resumes almost prior resting values for about 0.3 second. Thereafter the EMG resumes peaking values of 4 to 26, which outlast the right EEG by 3.8 second. With minor differences the values of the EEG correspond with those on the right.

Figure 12. Tracings from spontaneous, unstimulated movements in unanesthetized cat unrestrained in cage. Electrodes in right prerolandic hind-paw region, confirmed upon stimulation. Upper two EEG tracings are photographic recordings from oscillographic light beam movements, employing direct current amplification. The uppermost tracing is from right motor cortex, the tracing below is from left motor cortex. The lower two tracings are bipolar EMG from platinum iridium needle electrodes (both) in the leg extensor muscles in the left thigh. Of these the upper tracing (third from the top) represents a frequency range on the order of 50 to 500 cps. The lowermost tracing is made with the neurovoltmeter, registering the muscle potentials averaged at each instant. The EMG is seen to begin as soon as the corresponding EEG increase. Thereafter, while the bipolar EMG generally continues at high microvoltages, both right and left EEG with minor differences vary together as described in text.

During this (high EMG) interval the EEG has returned to prior resting values.

As in records previously examined in this chapter, evidence is lacking that this cat's brain began to function in the right prerolandic region prior to the onset of the left hind paw muscular region. However, there is no lag in the onset of the EEG that would suggest (as in the tracings of Bates) that the brain recordings are of proprioceptive origin. Contrariwise, a later record (not shown) from the same animal under similar conditions shows the onset of the EEG prior to the corresponding EMG.

In Mental Activities

Most of our tracings with our human and animal subjects show simultaneous onset of EMG and corresponding EEG or else prior onset of the former. Only a small minority show prior onset of the EEG. This is evidence against the traditional view that the brain *commands* (in the words of Paillard) the muscles. Indeed, the current view of "brain control," as said previously, rests on false premises. That impulses along fibers from large and small Betz cells lead to synaptic connections with other efferent fibers and these with still others leading in motor end-plates in muscles is unquestioned. That stimulation anywhere along these motor pathways results in contraction of some muscle fibers also is unquestioned. What has been unwarranted has been the common inference that these facts prove *brain control* of muscles along with the inference that mental activities, including moments of attention, recall, imagination, etc., are functions in and of the brain exclusively. So universally is this belief disseminated that the scientific as well as the lay public believe it as once they believed that the earth is flat.

What evidence I have reviewed in this chapter speaks to the contrary. As Sherrington and Setschenow hinted, all brain sections eventually lead to muscle. In unanesthetized animals, Ewald has shown that stimulation of the cortex anywhere produces movement.[22] Accordingly the physiological interconnec-

---

[22] TALBERT, G. A.: Über Rindenreizung am freilaufenden Hunde nach, J. R. Ewald. *Arch. Anat. Physiol.*, Leipzig, 1900, 24:195-208 (quoted by R. W. Doty).

tions between brain and muscle are evidenced as stated herein above.

The present investigations over a thirty-five year period lead me to conclude that in moments of mental activity specific brain action is a necessary but not by itself a sufficient condition. All our evidence points to the interpretation that the physiological circuits responsible for mental activity patterns are not closed in the brain, as still is commonly presumed, but pass to and fro. Central and peripheral patterns thus are as inextricably interconnected as in our telephone systems.

For convenience in referring to this type of interconnection, I have suggested the phrase, *reciprocating activation* (*R.A.*). It is hoped that future investigations the world over will throw light on this subject, providing quantitative information.

Brain investigators face still another problem. Why is it that we can record the peripheral patterns in mental activity with precision (provided that we have electronic apparatus of sufficient stability and sensitivity to record low voltage transients) but that the central brain pattern corresponding there-to most often elude us? The explanation which seems to me to cover the findings of investigators up to date, including myself, is quite unexpected.

EEG Not Correlated With Behavior Patterns Nor to Emotional and Other Mental Activities

First, what in general are the pertinent findings of other investigators? In a splendid review entitled "Electroencephalographic Correlates of Conditioned Responses," C. E. Wells concludes as follows: "While these investigations have emphasized the involvement of multiple structures within the nervous system in even the simplest sensory associations, they have as yet been unable to associate changes in the electrical activity of the brain with overt behavioral manifestations. Almost no one has asserted that the electroencephalographic changes observed with juxtaposed stimuli bear any direct relation to the behavioral activity of the animal. We are thus faced with the overriding problem of relating changes in the brain's electrical activity to the subject's behavior."[23]

---

[23] GLASER, G. H. (Ed.): *EEG and Behavior.* New York, Basic Books, 1963, p. 95,

The words quoted above would apply equally to the results of EEG investigations up to date if we replace the word "behavior" with the words, "emotional and other mental states."[24]

We now face the overriding problem of relating changes in the brain's electrical activity to mental moments, including emotional ones. In vernacular terms, I venture to suggest that we "have been barking up the wrong tree"! Speaking only for myself, I recall that, ever since the early 1920s, when Hans Berger and I were engaged in a race unknown to each other to be the first to measure brain voltages—a race which he won—I have assumed that an identifiable, specific brain pattern characterized each mental moment. Only recently I have begun to doubt this, leaving aside reflexive and sensory neuronal patterns.

In Every Mental Activity What is Specific is the Neuromuscular Pattern

Instead, as the result of experiments of others and of myself, including particularly those reviewed in this chapter, I am inclined to the opposite belief, surprising as this may at first seem. According to the ultrasensitive measurements during mental activities which have been continued almost daily in my laboratory these past thirty-five years, a specific neuromuscular pattern marks the character of each and every moment of their occurrence. The assumption that there is an equally specific and as readily recordable central pattern has not borne fruit, excepting in a minority of recordings. No one has produced such recordings in convincing measure.

Among the outstanding contributions thereon have been those of Jasper and Penfield. These authors have published the excellent specimens reproduced in Figures 7 and 8. However, these authors themselves cast doubt on the common belief that the motor centers before and behind the rolandic cortex really control voluntary motor activities. Instead they regard the prero-

---

[24] For lack of space herein, a review of the many investigations bearing on the EEG of mental activities will be postponed to a later volume to be intitled *Physiological Psychiatry*.

landic cortex as a "motor way station." To them, higher centers in the brain stem, which Penfield calls *centrencephalic,* account for the initiation of voluntary motor activities.

The Brain Pattern is often Nonspecific

Leaving their important suggestions for testing and possible confirmation to future investigations, I here go further, suggesting that the nature of mental activities can be accounted for and depends upon specific recordable and repeatable neuromuscular patterns; however, that the brain pattern is nonspecific in the sense that often if not always it may vary even when the neuromuscular pattern is distinctive and is repeated, as in the act of imagining, let us say, the Eiffel Tower in Paris or rowing a boat.[25]

Theory of Common Nonspecific Brain Action Patterns

This suggestion contradicts what I have long expected to find in EEG recordings during mental activities, including those accompanying voluntary movements. Doubtless, as well, it contradicts the expectations and predictions of other physiologists. But as I have become accustomed to this changed postulate, its probability has seemed to grow in my estimation. If we consider the telephone system, often compared with the nervous system, although with striking differences, we may be helped in the present comparison. What goes on in a telephone conversation between two individuals at different phones? Verbal signals pass between them. This is what constitutes the specific section of the connections employed. Please note that connecting the two phones can be performed automatically or by a personal central operator in many more than one specific pattern of central operations.

What takes place that is specific is at the periphery, namely the telephone, which in our simile corresponds with the peripheral neuromuscular connections. "Central" makes the connections variously in nonspecific, nonrepeatable patterns.

In short, in the past we have underestimated the complexity of

---

[25] *Loc. cit.,* 1-7, p. 4-A.

the brain in our preconceptions. We have assumed that the brain patterns will and must be specific for each and every individuated mental moment. The assumption proves only partly justified. Future EEG investigations on mental activities should be set on the revised track.[26]

We conclude, then, that the brain pattern in any individual at any moment of some type of mental activity often is nonspecific and thus, since the neuromuscular activity generally is quite specific, it is more readily identifiable and measureable and will stamp the thumbprint.

---

[26] In harmony with the findings and views set forth above, is the following statement by A. Fessard: "They (cybernetic schemata) aid us to escape at one and the same time both the naivétes of strict localizationism and the confusions of integral holisticism" (Le conditionnement considere l' echelle du neurone. Suppl. 13, *Int. J. Electroenceph. Clin. Neurol.*, Mont., 1960, p. 157).

Bearing upon brain patterns and specific localization is the following significant comment by H. Jasper, G. Ricci and B. Doane: "The microelectrode view of changes in patterns of neuronal firing in response to an alerting stimulus or to a motor response emphasizes the fact that all parts of the brain are in continuous activity in the alert animal, in a situation in which he is ready to respond to avoid an unpleasant stimulus" (Microelectrode analysis of cortical cell discharge during avoidance conditioning in the monkey, *ibid.*, p. 152.

Chapter VIII

PRESENTING NEW PRINCIPLES OF EMOTION

SECTION A—EMOTION AND THE SPASTIC DIGESTIVE TRACT

THE INFLUENCE of acute emotional states on the digestive tract has long been recognized. As noted on previous pages, it was exemplified in cats and dogs particularly by Walter Cannon. Clinicians commonly associate mucous colitis with the spastic colon and chronic nervous and emotional states. In a previous monograph, I have discussed this subject, including the diagnosis.[1] This should be familiar material to the therapist who deals continually with hyperemotional states. Anxiety states are characterized by spasticity of the digestive tract.

Spastic esophagus was considered by Harlow Brooks to be the most common malady of mankind.[2] The diagnosis may be clearly indicated by a history of dysphagia, if no local organic pathology is demonstrable. However, in most instances seen by the therapist, no history of difficulty in swallowing will be elicited. More often, complaint is made of substernal pressure or vague distress. The physician may think of coronary insufficiency. In a discussion of this subject, I have pointed out that spasm of the esophagus commonly accompanies signs of coronary insufficiency.[3] In consequence, physicians commonly ascribe the pressure or semi-choking sensation to the heart, when really it derives from the spastic esophagus. This confusion is the more difficult to avoid if, as I venture to opine, the esophagus will be found to be more or

---

[1] JACOBSON, E.: Spastic esophagus and mucous colitis. *Arch. Intern. Med. (Chicago)*, 39:433-435, Mar., 1927.

[2] H. BROOKS in Tiel's *Practise of Medicine*, 7 (Medicine), 1921, Chapter X, p. 379. His statement was made in a medical lecture.

[3] JACOBSON, E.: Principles underlying coronary heart disease. *Cardiologia*, 26,2:83-102, 1955.

less spastic at times in most or in all instances of coronary insufficiency as well as of anxiety reaction. This result can be expected from reflex effects due to coronary insufficiency, with accompanying side-effects on the esophagus of emotional derivation. This will be discussed further in the following section of this chapter.

Roentgenological diagnosis of spasticity of the esophagus is made with barium paste, (page 129). Commonly, the spasticity includes the cardia, with delayed emptying time. The esophagus is so responsive to emotional states that it often becomes temporarily spastic in healthy subjects. Accordingly, to determine enduring or chronic spasm may require repeated tests by the one-swallow method.

Spastic Stomach

Spasticity of the stomach is somewhat more difficult to discriminate. Under fluoroscopy or in films, the hook-shape or other contour suggests steady contraction of the muscular walls and/or hyperperistalsis. Emptying time is delayed upon persistent contraction of the pyloric sphincter. Ulcer and other local pathology must be ruled out if the spasticity is to be ascribed chiefly to emotional states. Yet peptic ulcer, as I suggested in 1929, is a feature of tension disorder.

The diagnosis of spasticity of the colon rests chiefly upon the history, the character of the stools, the findings upon abdominal palpation and the roentgenological examination. Commonly, the patient suffering with chronic anxiety relates of chronic constipation or of recurrent loose stools or both conditions more or less alternately. In many instances there is complaint of recurrent distress in the abdomen. This may appear in the lower portion, transversely or at the sides. The distress bears no constant time relation to meals.

Spastic Colon

Palpation with the palm of the examiner's hand resting lightly but flat on the abdomen enables the form, resistance and tenderness of the colon at any point to be estimated. Upon mild but deep pressure, wincing or a facial expression of distress is elicited at tender points, often including the caecum, the hepatic and/or splenic flexure and/or the rectum. Likewise, the intestinal content may be estimated in some instances as a movable mass.

The form of the stools, when not soft or liquid, is thin, cigarette or cigar-shaped, or in small pellets or balls. In any event, it gives the impression of constriction. A coating of mucus may often be noted. If hemorrhoids are present, the constricted stools may be marked with fresh blood. Purulent complications are noted but seldom. The diagnosis then may be ulcerative colitis.

In order to secure a view of the colon at length, fluoroscopy should be performed about eight to twelve hours after a barium meal. Cathartics and sedatives and if possible other medication should be avoided for at least twenty-four hours before the meal. Palpation under the x-ray should be deferred until a photograph has been taken. Increased peristalsis often is apparent. The films show irregular haustration with deepening thereof. Most apparent may be chronic spasm evidenced by absence of the barium in sections of the colon at irregular intervals, while the colon which appears shows increased and striking variation in contour and in volume in one place or another along its course. Complete blockage may be ascribed to spasm, but sometimes it is wise to test whether this disappears if atropine is administered in sufficient dosage. Thus diverticulae, polyps and other tumors, including malignant ones, can be ruled out. Except for this purpose, barium enemas and air insufflation can be omitted in anxiety states.

Since spasticity of the colon may result reflexly from local inflammations and other irritative sources, including tumors and traumata, differential diagnosis is always necessary. This need not be discussed here, since the distinguishing marks of organic disease of the digestive tract can be found in texts on that subject. These comments will apply likewise to the discussion of spastic esophagus and stomach which follows.

SECTION B—EVALUATION A PRINCIPAL FUNCTION OF EMOTION

What was said in the preceding section on spastic colon marking anxiety and other emotional states is no longer new, and to a large extent has gained general acceptance among physicians. It was set forth in 1929 in my monograph, *Progressive Relaxation*. However, when first I presented the matter in the section on gastroenterology at the annual meeting of the American Medical Association, a surgeon objected that the roentgen films indicated the need for operation. Fortunately, I was able to reply that my associates also had passed upon the films and that they included a surgeon of national prominence.

In the present pages, it is necessary to present additional features of emotion which may strike many readers as no less novel. In any event, they are based upon forty years of clinical and laboratory research. During this long period of investigation, I have prized observations first and theories second. Thus, the views presented here have virtually been forced upon me by the realities which I have been obliged to face. Objectively, I have been guided by the results of the methods outlined in previous chapters. Subjectively, I have trained my subjects to report technically on their experiences. They have learned the elements of what in earlier chapters was termed *internal communication*. Let me hasten to say that teaching them to be observers has been no easy task for them or for me. The principles of this training have been indicated previously.[4] The methods have been improved on those which I have used in the training of graduate students, some of whom subsequently have become professors and chairmen in university departments of psychology. Commonly, the laboratory and clinical subjects of the present investigation have shown skill, accuracy and scientific impartiality.

Previous writers have approached the subject of emotion chiefly from certain limited viewpoints, namely, (a) the peripheral organs and glands involved or (b) the time-relations (Lange, James) or (c) the nerve centers in action (Cannon) or (d) the psychoanalytic origin and meaning. Some of their contributions have been outstanding. However, it remains to show what emotion does for man chiefly.

---

[4] JACOBSON, E.: On meaning and understanding. *Amer. J. Psychol., XXII:* 533-537, 1911.

Emotion Has Function

Emotion is not only being "moved" physiologically: *Emotion is the framework in which man apprehends reality.* It is evaluation of the situation with which he is confronted. Until we understand this, we have failed to comprehend the role of emotion. The bare data of the physiological laboratory will leave us gaping in our ignorance.

The skeleton of emotions, so to speak, has been well investigated in animals and in man. We come now to the flesh and blood. When man is angry or afraid, joyous or in tears, he is not only apprehending reality or what he takes to be reality but also is evaluating it. For him the evaluation often is most important.

By no means is this view wholly foreign to the extensive literature on emotion. Quite the opposite is true. Psychiatrists who have studied the schizophrenic reaction have witnessed the failure to grasp reality when appropriate emotional response is pathologically absent. The well-known theory of attention held by E. B. Titchener and many other psychologists of his day dwelt on the indispensible role of interest. Other examples could be cited to the effect that the role of emotion in the apprehension of reality has not been altogether neglected.

Evaluation of Stimuli

Be this as it may, we come to a fresh and useful point of view if we clearly recognize that *in many respects the most important function of emotion is evaluation of reality.*[5]

---

[5] In harmony with this conclusion are the following comments of E. Gellhorn concerning integrations performed by the nervous system: "According to Ward and McCulloch, cortico-hypothalamic connections are restricted to the frontal lobe. If this is the case it must be assumed that the transmission of impulses from the primary sensory projection areas to the frontal lobes precedes emotional excitement based on a sensory impression; or, to express this matter in simple psychological terms, the *evaluation* of sensory experience by the frontal lobes is a prerequisite of an emotional arousal on a sensory basis. Such an interpretation is not without experimental foundation. The separation of connections between the frontal lobe and the thalamus and hypothalamus as practiced in frontal lobotomy has been shown to decrease or eliminate the emotional reactivity to severe pain (Freeman and Watts, Falconer). However it is likely that the activation of the hypothalamus from sensory projection areas via the frontal lobes plays a role only in primates." (WARD, A. A.,

In this sense, the doctor should be prepared to understand anxiety and to treat it with the means at his disposal. He should recognize that *emotion is as emotion does*. This applies to anxiety no less than to any other emotional state. Schematic diagrams are offered in Figures 3 and 4.

Since each state of emotion, including anxiety, is a constantly changing kaleidoscope of images and motor reactions, unique at each and every moment in any individual, we need to inquire what our patient feels and does and include our objective tests and measurements whenever possible. When we become aware that each anxious state in our patients is unique, like each individual painting of an artist, we will be better prepared to meet their needs.

In this sense, we repeat that *anxiety is as anxiety does* and inquire about what our anxious patients are really trying to do.

The Cause of Emotion

The anxious person commonly attributes his state to some cause or causes, which are of many varieties. His concern may relate to finances, personal relations, health, home, children or other rela-

---

JR., and McCULLOCH, W. S.: The projection of the frontal lobe on the hypothalamus, *J. Neurophysiol.*, 10:309-314, 1947; FREEMAN, W., and WATTS, J. W.: Pain of organic disease relieved by prefrontal lobotomy. *Lancet* 1:953-955, 1946; FALCONER, M. A.: Relief of intractable pain of organic origin by frontal lobectomy. *Res. Publ. Ass. Nerv. Ment. Dis.*, 27:706-714, 1948).

Also in harmony with the conclusion that emotion has to do with evaluation are the following comments of J. Elkes: "As in the case of other modalities (for example, muscle tone, or posture, or fine voluntary movement), the deliberate selection (by experimental intervention) of one "bit" of behavior from a larger repertoire in no way reflects the elegance, smoothness, and flow of the normal operation. What normally manifests, what finally is selected out, or, as we say, what we experience represents in fact, a final common path. Yet the activation of such an affective response, and the genetically programmed cell assembly which subserves it, is presumably preceded, within fractions of a second, by several simultaneous transactions involving the temporal apposition, convergence, and coding of neural patterns at widely separated topographical levels. It may, for example, involve the taking in of sensory cues (or the activation of a memory trace); the analysis and matching of these in terms of cognate traces, or, as we say "experience"; a grouping and further condensation of these transforms in terms of their appetitive (YES) or aversive (NO) connotation; and the final activation of the appropriate motor-somato-endocrine response" (ELKES, J.: In SIMON, A. [Ed.]: *The Physiology of Emotions*, Springfield, Thomas, 1961, pp. 102-103). The passages quoted above appear elsewhere in this volume, but are repeated because of their significance for neuropsychiatry.

tives, country, guilt, failures, life or death and other matters in countless variations and details. He may be worried about himself or about others close to him. All degrees of selfishness may appear and even of altruism, although altruistic anxiety is less common.

Removing the Cause

Generally, the anxious person is prone to believe that the matter of his concern causes his emotion and that this would subside with the removal or rectification of the cause. Accordingly, his efforts extend toward seeking relief or in reflecting on what might have been. Thus, states of neuromuscular tension arise varying from moment to moment, giving anxiety its variegated subjective character and outward behavior; but always the effort-tension is to solve the problem and to achieve thereby the goal of relief. To do so the anxious person feels prompted, even more or less compelled. This is the core of the physiological psychiatry of anxiety. So much we can recognize clearly and, knowing this, the therapist can be prepared as a rule to take steps toward effective relief of the anxiety. Not knowing this, he may be tempted to speculative explanations of the anxious state, which then baffles him.

There is a second temptation which the therapist can learn to resist. It is the temptation to agree with the patient and the family who "know" that if the "cause" of the anxiety is removed, the patient will return to "normal." The therapist dealing with chronic anxiety cannot always agree with this tempting assumption scientifically. For example, a woman suffering from persistent anxiety asserted that it was caused by the pastor of the Episcopalian church to which she was devoted. She and her husband reasoned that for seven years they had listened to this pastor without edification and that if now she would change her attendance to another church of her denomination, she would "remove the cause" of her emotional difficulties.

Needless to say to the experienced reader, no such easy remedy brings long existing habits of overanxiety to an abrupt, successful termination. The belief of the patient with its autosuggestive implications soon proves ineffectual.

When the individual perceives and evaluates, he commonly ascribes certain features to the situations and the problems which he faces. These vary with his anxious state or other mood, but often he does not realize this. Freudians might say that he "projects." Failure to discriminate tension pattern clearly from objective reality is distinctive of anxiety and other emotion reactions.

Obviously, the attempt to solve the problems underlying the anxieties of life, thereby to relieve concern, extends from Zeno to Hamlet in all of us. Without doubt, anxiety is useful insofar as it leads man to recall and to reflect and to foresee, and thus to avoid misfortune and to assure greater adaptive success. In the last century a noted writer asserted that fear thus is the springboard of all education.

However, there is such a thing as becoming too tense in the efforts of anxiety. Man's quest for security can lead him too far, with the loss of other goods. He can become overanxious!

SECTION C—EMOTION IS PARTLY PASSIVE (SMOOTH AND CARDIAC MUSCULATURE) PARTLY ACTIVE (STRIATED MUSCULATURE)

While most accounts of emotion give the chief roles to smooth and cardiac musculature, some others recognize that the striated musculature participates also, at least to some extent.

We can begin our outline of the role of muscle by considering first the smooth and cardiac varieties.

Smooth Muscle Response

The participation of smooth muscle in emotion is copiously illustrated in investigations on animals and on man. Cannon's classical studies on laboratory animals have been mentioned above.[6] In man, each portion of the digestive tract appears to play a distinctive role in the emotional life of man.

A fly alighting on the nose of the subject occasioned a tightening of the esophageal musculature in the laboratory of Arnold Luckhardt. Every emotional response was marked by a tighten-

---

[6] CANNON, W. B.: Bodily Changes in Pain, Hunger, Fear and Rage. New York, Appleton, 2nd ed., 1929.

ing or relaxation. My own studies with a condom in the esophagus (a procedure introduced by Walter Cannon) confirmed the results of Luckhardt. The muscular changes occur in the smooth as well as in the striated musculature in healthy man. From muscle, afferent nerves convey a general feeling of substernal "tightness" or "pressure" which varies with the muscular portion of the esophagus which contracts. Thus the experience of anxiety or other emotion is a composite of great subjective variation and complexity. Each one of us has a world of experience within ourselves which passes unobserved yet influences our every impulse, decision and act. While unobserved, it is well to repeat that these experiences are conscious.

In chronic anxiety states the roentgenological film taken five minutes after the one-swallow test may reveal fairly persistent and characteristic configurations in the esophagus. For example, often seen is the V-shaped bolus.[7] It may persist for hours. As previously set forth, this is the physiological basis of the "globus hystericus" of classical neurology.

To the self-observing doctor, sensations from his own esophagus should be an open book. He might recognize them during any period of difficult study, such as solving problems of calculus or other mathematics. When effort fails to bring the solution, the esophagus often clutches automatically. Realizing only the objective difficulty encountered, the student often will quit the task for a time, driven by the clutching esophagus, though he knows it not. How often have I had this experience, realizing it only after I have recessed!

Dysphagia

Accordingly in many cases of chronic anxiety, the outstanding symptom becomes dysphagia. Often the patient consults the doctor with this chief complaint. Current treatment is by prescription of sedatives or tranquilizers. Less often, calcium salts are administered. In severe instances, olives on rubber catheters are passed to distend the walls. I have discussed the symptoms, the

---

[7] JACOBSON, E.: *Progressive Relaxation.* Chicago, U. of Chicago, rev. ed., 1938, p. 364.

etiology and the treatment by relaxation methods previously.[8]

If the anxiety of the patient is carried in the stomach muscula-ture, the spasticity may prove incompatible with adequate circu-lation to the mucosa. Possibly some such factor facilitates the formation of ulcer. A suggestion to this effect first appeared in my *Progressive Relaxation* in 1929. This suggestion appeared to take hold in the medical profession, supplanting previous views. However, it remained for a distinguished surgeon, Dr. Lester Dragstedt, to bring forth the evidence. This he did by severing the vagus nerve and showing the consequent increased healing and lessened recurrence of peptic ulcer.[9]

The influence of emotion on the stomach was the subject of the classic studies of Stewart Wolf and H. G. Wolff.[10]

Colonic Response

Like the esophagus and the stomach, the colon displays dis-tinctive high tension contours in anxiety states. In many in-stances, the patient experiences the spasticity in sensations so vague and ill-defined as to surpass his powers of description. Commonly, he complains of loose movements or of constipation or of alternating forms. Often, however, he visits his general practitioner or internist or surgeon with complaints of abdominal distress which interfere with his daily goals. Sometimes the sur-geon operates, as Dr. Evarts Graham of St. Louis discussed and condemned.

When distress from any part of the digestive tract becomes sufficiently severe to excite attention, the spasticity exceeds the

[8] JACOBSON, E.: Voluntary relaxation of the esophagus. *Amer. J. Physiol.*, 72:387-394, May, 1925; JACOBSON, E.: Spastic esophagus and mucous colitis. *Arch. Intern. Med. (Chicago)*, 39:433-445, March, 1927.

[9] DRAGSTEDT, L. R., PALMER, W. L., SCHAFER, P. W., HODGES, P. C.: Super-diaphragmatic section of vagus nerves in treatement of duodenal and gastric ulcers. *Gastroenterology*, 3:450-462, Dec., 1944; DRAGSTEDT, L. R., and SCHAFER, P. W.: Removal of vagus innervation of stomach in gastroduodenal ulcer. *Surgery*, 17: 742-749, May, 1945.

[10] WOLFF, HAROLD G., and WOLF, STEWART: Studies on a subject with a large gastric fistula: Changes in the function of the stomach in association with varying emotional states. *Trans. Amer. Ass. Physicians*, 57: 115, 1942; WOLF, STEWART, and WOLFF, H. G.: *Human Gastric Function: An Experimental Study of Man and His Stomach.* New York, Oxford U. P., 1943.

bounds of emotional experience. The distress and the condition become an objective matter for attention and concern. Often the anxious person thus is complex in his emotion. The anxiety, so to speak, bears compound interest.

In all events, the presence of spasticity in any portion of the digestive tract will inevitably be one mark of anxiety. Nevertheless, the cautious physician will think of differential diagnosis.

As is well known to surgeons, spasticity in portions of the digestive tract marks the presence of local pathology, including inflammation, tumors and occasionally lesions of the spinal cord or other nerve pathways. Spasticity arising under such etiological conditions does not result afferently in the experience of anxiety.

Anxiety Response and the Digestive Tract

During anxiety, we may consider the spastic configuration of the digestive tract as the result of reflex influences. In terms of physiologic tension control, reflex influences are coordinate with *automatic controls*. Other examples of automatic controls are the actions of enzymes, hormones and other chemical agents in the body. Such agents possibly are active in anxiety, but controlled investigation is needed.

More frequently studied have been the reactions of the blood vessels, as in flushing or in heightened blood pressure during anxious or other severe emotion. Increased rate of the heart beat along with increased respiratory rate is a matter of common observation. These changes underlie the familiar lie detector tests, which include also the psychogalvanic reflex. While this reflex, as well as perspiration and salivation, have been set forth by some authors as measurements of emotion, the view has been challenged and cannot be regarded as established.

Automatic Responses

In animals, piloerection and contraction of the nictitating membrane are familiar marks of emotion, as are sudden pupil changes in man. Increased white cell count and eosinophilia are often referred to.[11] These again are examples of reflex effects

---

[11] See Chapter III for other phenomena in animals.

or automatic controls in anxiety and other emotional states. In other words, the smooth muscle and other reflex effects during emotion are the passive aspect of that universal experience in man.

Striated Muscles Active in Emotion

The significance of striated muscle action in each and every kind of emotional state has not received due recognition. To be sure, general psychologists, including William James, stressed the participation of striated musculature in all emotional states. However, he never seemed to realize that, in view of this participation, emotion should not be regarded as purely passive.

Even less attention to the role of the striated musculature in emotion has been given by writers and practitioners of psychiatry. Nevertheless, to the extent that striated muscle action participates in every moment of emotion, the latter is a voluntary act of the organism. This fact has been largely neglected even by university psychologists. It means that our emotions have definitive ends or goals in the same fashion (even if not to the same full extent) as do our efforts.

Efforts and Goals not Separate Occurrences

We should recognize that, in the intact organism, efforts and emotions and their respective goals do not occur apart from each other as separate occurrences. It is the psychologist with his verbalisms who effects the dichotomy. Concretely, the goal of an effort is no different from the goal of the emotion which marks the effort.

Insofar as our efforts at any moment are constituted physiologically by patterns of skeletal muscle contraction and relaxation, they are under a different form of control from patterns of smooth and cardiac muscle contraction. For this reason, psychologists are accustomed to classify acts in which striated muscle plays a dominant role as "voluntary" whereas the participation of the two other muscular types are termed "involuntary." Employing these terms in the customary sense, we now conclude that *emotion is never completely involuntary.*

If this is true, the view that emotion is quite involuntary which largely prevails in psychology and in psychiatry can no longer be regarded as fully supported.

Increased Action-Potentials Levels

That striated muscle action occurs during varied or all types of emotional states has been illustrated in action-potential studies in my laboratory almost daily for many years. In severe anxiety states, acute or chronic, high readings in microvolts are noted from electrodes in or over every striated muscle tested. The test can be made in any muscle of the extremities, legs, trunk, neck or head. With subsidence of the emotional state, as reported by the trained subject, and with diminution of the behavior patterns of emotion, the action-potentials decrease likewise, and vice versa.

These findings apply if the apparatus employed has sufficiently low voltage sensitivity, stability of recording and low noise to signal ratios. The voltage sensitivity needed is at the least one centimeter per microvolt excursion by the recorder. I have been called in consultation about commercial apparatus purchased in university departments intended for these psychological pur-poses but which lacks sufficient low voltage sensitivity, and I must warn accordingly. For descriptions of technique along with required control tests, the reader is referred to previous publica-tions.[12]

We can go still further in the interpretation and formulation of our findings. Let us begin by recalling the peripheral phenomena of vast variety and extent which numerous investigators have ob-served and recorded in emotional states of man and of animals.[13]

Every Effort is Distinguished by a
Striated Muscle Tension-Pattern

The physiological picture in effort states is less well known, for previously it has not been as adequately described as has emotion. Effort states, we are led to assume, are distinguished by the pres-ence of patterns of striated muscular contraction. Reflex reactions likewise are so distinguished, but these are stereotyped acts which

---

[12] JACOBSON, E., An Integrating Voltmeter for the Study of Nerve and Muscle Potentials, Rev. of Scientific Instruments, 11(12): 415-418, Dec. 1940.

[13] Chapter III.

can be elicited repeatedly by appropriate stimulation. Effort states cannot thus be elicited in stereotyped fashion. Furthermore, even in the same individual under controlled conditions, effort states tend to show variety and change upon repetition, whereas reflex action tends to be monotonously repeatable and duplicable.

Anatomically, reflex reaction has been investigated by a long line of eminent physiologists, including Keith Lucas and Charles Sherrington. The neuromuscular channels often have been ascertained and their repetitive employment in a particular type of reflex has been demonstrated. The usefulness of deep tendon reflexes was for a long time dubious, until Paul Hoffmann showed that effortful acts such as walking owe their coordination and engineered smoothness to the participation of reflex action.[14]

Efforts Involve the Entire Organism

We assume that the striated muscular contraction characteristic in any effort state occurs with participation of impulses to the muscle along motor nerves (and with acetylcholine or other chemical action at the end-plates) and from the muscle along afferent nerves. Likewise, we assume that in effort states there is concomitant activity in the central nervous system including the brain, without which there would be no neuromuscular action in the intact vertebrate. Furthermore we do not exclude from effort states the indispensible action of heart and blood vessels in establishing and maintaining the blood pressure and circulation required for sustained striated muscle action. In effort states, also, we assume that the vegetative nervous system plays an essential role, even if less prominent than in emotion.

The Effort Circuit

Taking the above mentioned neuromuscular, central nervous, vegetative nervous and cardiovascular systems into account, we can include all this varied, kaleidoscopic physiologic participation under the term, *effort-circuit*. Years of research by numerous

---

[14] HOFFMANN, PAULS "Die Physiologischerv Eigenschaften der Eigenreflexe. *Ergebn. Physiol.* 36:13-108, 1934.

investigators will be required before we can learn as much about effort circuits as now we know about reflex circuits; but a firm beginning has been made. Much more must be investigated concerning the participation of the endocrine system as well as the character of the basic chemistry.

Recalling what has been said above about the participation of of striated muscle during emotion as well as during effort states, we can be prepared to regard each and every emotion as to some extent part and parcel of an effort or a set of efforts.

Effort in Emotion

Emotion, including anxiety, always makes up part of an effort state. If this view is sound, it will be supported upon investigation by methods of physiological psychiatry. In this, the subject trained in the method of autosensory observation and report will supply more reliable data than if not trained. Evidence will be indicated that, in each emotional act, the individual strives for some attainment at the same moment as he feels himself more or less passive in the grip of the emotion. In numerous such studies, I have found supporting evidence of this ambivalence of effort activity and passive reception.

Chapter IX

PRESENTING FURTHER NEW PRINCIPLES
OF EMOTION

SECTION A—THE ROLE OF IMAGERY IN EMOTION

Inciting Role of Images

For the most part overlooked in theories of the emotions and in clinical neuropsychiatry is *the inciting role* of imagery. In my opinion, if this function of imagery is neglected, the principles of emotion cannot be understood, and therefore psychiatry cannot be practised adequately.

The role of imagery is reported by subjects educated to observe what was called the internal code in an earlier chapter. What follows is a summary based upon controlled neuropsychiatric observation and reporting by such trained subjects over a period of forty years.

Observing Images

Commonly, the subject readily learns to recognize and to report the imagery present during emotional states, including anxiety. Examples will be recounted in later chapters which relate to individual patients. As a rule, the patient pictures the matter of his concern or something clearly related thereto. At times, the visual image may be fairly static for a sustained period, while, at others, the imagery changes from moment to moment. Generally, there is no single image which marks an anxiety state, but rather a whole set of varied imagery. The subject sees various objects in imagination, always in one or another line of his visual axis, with or without fluctuations over a brief period of seconds or less. Therewith occur sensations from the extraocular muscles as of looking in one direction or another or in changing directions. Therewith also occurs inner speaking. This can consist of fairly

136

clear inner articulatory processes in sentence form. Often, however, the sentences are abortive. The wording may be sparse and repetitious. In all events, the individual words are likely to be abbreviated and in telescoped or "shorthand" form. Auditory imagery may or may not be reported in addition.

It is of the utmost importance that the doctor understand the function of imagery in the life of the individual, including his goals as well as his acts. In brief, images are tools for effective action and reaction. They are part of the mechanisms employed for the internal *representation* of reality without or within the organism and what is to be done about it. This includes fantasy, and in pathological states, illusion, delusion and hallucination. Images are internal signals.

Imagery in Anxiety

Aside from ocular and speech representation, other form of action and reaction are common in anxiety and other emotional states. They are essential components and the doctor can profit from examining them during his own experiences of anxiety. Their number and variety are legion. Any neuromuscular portion of the organism may participate in the play of emotion. The function of these components, along with that of visual, speech, auditory and other imagery, is representation by the *organism to the organism.* However hasty, vague and fragmentary their representative signals, what they characterize are the past, present, future, possible and fancied aspects of situations to be met as well as the manner of this meeting. Thus, the anxiety state is by turns reminiscent, perceptive, prophetic or fantastic or all these together at one moment. The patient may report sensations as from muscular tension in one portion of his body or another as if to reminisce, perceive, prophesy or fancy. If we were to compare the anxiety state with a sunset, we might say that generally it is less static, less beautiful, but extremely more complex in its manifold changes.

Imagery Ignored

Nevertheless, as a rule throughout the experience and its recurrences, a somewhat constant or continual form of representation of the matter of concern is constituted by the visual imagery. Commonly, the partially trained subject is so lost in the meaning of his thought and in the goal that the imagery itself is ignored. Only as he becomes a skilled observer does he begin to recognize the visual and the speech imagery along with the variegated sensations from muscular tensions and from other bodily component processes. In severe anxiety, action-potential recordings reveal increased values from diverse portions of the neuromusculature. Indeed, if the emotion is active, the recordings generally are high from any muscular region whatsoever which the operator selects.

The Effort Circuit Includes Imagery

All that is said above can be included in one comprehensive term, *the effort circuit*. However, the doctor who employs this term should be aware that much more is comprehended than participation of the nervous system alone. There is no effort that does not occur in a network of vital reflexes, particularly the cardiovascular and the respiratory. Likewise in the network are the gastrointestinal reflexes, as outlined in these chapters. Of so much we can be confident; but doubtless there is much more to be learned about glandular and chemical changes which future investigation may disclose as perhaps no less intrinsic to the effort mechanism.

Cautious Teaching

While training his patient to be a competent observer of the effort circuit, the cautious physician will avoid leading questions. Step by step he will lead his pupil to observe without bias. Before attempting to observe actions and reactions related to the matter of anxiety, training should be devoted to observations of neutral or more nearly indifferent affect.

How Anxiety May be Triggered

In general I have found that the anxiety state is very often adduced or triggered upon the occurrence of eye tensions and visual imagery. This is easy to understand. Just as man informs himself about his environment by vision, so he rehearses the past, indicates to himself the present and prophesies the future or distorts it in fancy through the same sort of sensory avenue. As I have shown, action of the extraocular muscles is indispensible in visualization. In addition to brain circuits, the individual employs his ocular apparatus as if looking at and in the direction of the object seen in imagination.[1] If he does not direct his eyes accordingly, he does not visualize.

Accordingly, we are led to apply the principles outlined on behalf of the mental welfare of the patient. We train him to the skill of noting the visual imagery present in anxiety and of the extraocular tensions present as if to look at objects of concern. If in addition he can learn to relax the extraocular tensions mentioned, we should expect that we have taken steps toward averting the occurrence of the anxiety.

We Do Not Alter the Objective Difficulty

Obviously, thereby we do not remove any situation which might to any extent have stimulated the anxiety. Instead, the instructor aims to show the anxious patient how to meet the situation with adaptive success. In so doing he need not and should not offer reassurance. It is not the instructor's mission to philosophize or to explain, e.g., that the problem faced is "not as bad as it seems." He is not to think for the patient nor to tell him what to do. I hope that the reader will enlist to outmode such current neuropsychiatric approaches.

The instructor in tension control, as will appear hereinafter, teaches his pupil, the patient, how to estimate his effort-costs and to effect economy in his energy outgo. He teaches certain principles bearing on the income/outgo ratio of human energies. The

---

[1] Forty years of controlled observation on patients and on healthy individuals, including myself, with the aid of objective techniques have convinced me that the participation of neuromuscular circuits in mental activities is a rule without exceptions. There are many other rules in physiology which likewise admit of no exceptions, although we may not think of them. For example, we *always* see with our eyes, hear with our auditory apparatus, breathe with our lungs. I cite these examples since I have met with physiologists who seem to have the impression that such terms as "for the most part" or "commonly" should be employed on all occasions.

teaching is simple. Farmers, laborers and mechanics learn readily, for the application is realistic as well as simple. I shall have more to say on saving of energies later.

Anxiety Control Depends on General Neuromusculature

Before closing this section, it should be stated that the patient is instructed in anxiety control not only through relaxation of trigger tensions of the ocular and speech apparatus. In addition he is drilled in the relaxation of the trunk regions, which include the respiratory apparatus directly and the visceral regions indirectly. Once more we recall that psychologists have recognized the participation of visceral sensations in emotions.[2] Cannon studied them objectively in animals, while I have studied them objectively in human beings, employing methods of roentgenology.[3] The anxious patient may report troublesome sensations, most often indicating regions of the stomach, duodenum, esophagus and/or colon. The trained patient discriminates sensations of tension as elements in his discomfort. These elements in his inner code he would gladly do without. Pharmaceutical houses vie with each other in producing a host of relaxants for the purposes mentioned. If the reader's patient has visited many doctors previously, he will be likely to have become a user (or victim) of one relaxant drug or another.

It should be emphasized over and over again that it will be a poor teacher of tension control who predicts relief to the patient, hoping to secure therapeutic results through therapeutic suggestion. Such methods, even if common in current medical practice, do not teach the patient to be self-reliant but rather to be dependent.

When the Patient Seeks Reassurance

Instead, no reassurance is offered. When the hypochondriac patient begs for reassurance, the instructor points out that his begging is an effortful act, in which tensions should be discriminated and relaxed systematically. No reader should assume that

---

[2] See Chapter VI.

[3] JACOBSON, E.: *Progressive Relaxation.* Chicago, U. of Chicago Press, rev. ed., 1938.

this instruction acts as a counter-suggestion, alleviating the discomfort hypnotically. Instead, let him try the pedagogy herein set forth, whereupon he will witness the development of skills of observation and of relaxation by the patient, step by step, rather than as a suggestive *fait accompli*. Better still, let him visit a clinic in which these methods are practiced meticulously.

In summary, the patient learns to indentify and discriminate the tension states of the trigger mechanisms of eyes and speech, but also of the trunk regions, including the respiratory and visceral (neuromuscular) tensions. He is drilled in relaxing the chief striated muscle groups singly and jointly. The smooth and cardiac neuromusculature cannot be relaxed directly, but responds reflexly with diminished tension upon progressive relaxation of the striated type. Such is the training if he is to learn progressive relaxation or self-operations control.

SECTION B—TYPES OF HUMAN IMAGERY

Since the days of Galton,[4] psychologists have believed that mankind can be divided into types in regard to the imagery employed. Thus, individuals can be said to employ chiefly visual or auditory or speech imagery. It has been agreed that some individuals lack visual imagery altogether.[5]

Normal Man Visualizes

Although I was brought up on this teaching, I have had to abandon it. The observations in almost daily teaching of patients for forty years have been responsible. So far as I know, no one previously has devoted this period of time to the field of imagery. My patients commonly have received instruction at least equivalent to graduate university training in autosensory

---

[4] GALTON, F.: *Inquiries into Human Faculty and Its Development.* New York, 1883. Earlier individual differences in imagination were studied by G. T. Feshner (*Elemente der Psychophysik,* 1860).

[5] According to William James, "*Some people undoubtedly have no visual images at all worthy of the name* [italics his] and instead of *seeing* their breakfast table, they tell you that they *remember* it or *know* what was on it." James ascribes this to verbal images. Evidently, James failed to realize that untrained observers are unreliable. *Principles of Psychology,* Vol. II. New York, Holt, 1907, pp. 57-58.

examination. They have included types who reported the absence of all visualization at first. However, without leading questions or suggestion, but with increasing skill at observation, these types begin to notice and to report cautiously. At first they tended to overlook images of vague and fleeting character, present possibly for only ten milliseconds or thereabouts (as I should conjecture in my own instance). Yet later, such fleeting imagery comes to be reported, although at first doubtfully. Finally, observation becomes firmer. We find that trained, experienced observation is as necessary in psychology as in pathology.

Such experiences in myself as in other highly experienced observers have led me to revise the classification of people as employing visual or motor types of imagery exclusively. The classification is not supported in my data. Apparently in *all* people except those born blind or without significant experience in vision, the visual image is present and tends to trigger emotional states, including anxiety. Imagologists, including J. R. Angell and others, have noted that modern education tends to promote the use of speech imagery to the point of substitution for visual imagery. Their point is well taken, for it is based upon observation and it is currently taught in college courses of psychology. However, we are obliged to modify their conclusions that the visual imagery really disappears. In this evidently they were mistaken. We find that the visual imagery does not wholly vanish; instead it becomes less vivid, less intense, but more transient and fleeting. A finer type of visual shorthand is developed in the highly educated. They retain the tool but refine it. In other words, they learn to employ less energy in their visualization. Thus, the visual imagery becomes less evident to the self-observer and he tends to overlook it unless he receives specialized instruction in autosensory observation.

Imageless Thought Nonexistent

According to the author's findings, then, "imageless thought" does not exist. It becomes apparent why the controversy over this matter raged among psychologists of an earlier epoch: Insufficient time was spent on the acquisition of skill of observation, particularly on the observation of faint and extremely brief imaginal phenomena. These were overlooked.

In summary, visualization in some is much more fleeting or transient and vague than in others, and the lack of sufficient training in the more advanced skills in autosensory examination evidently is what has led our predecessors to deny visualization in some classes of normal people.

SECTION C—RESIDUAL VISUALIZATION

Now we come to a new point, recently uncovered in our investigations of mental activities, including emotional states. For purposes of exposition I shall state the principle before proceeding to elucidate and cite evidence. The statement will not apply to those born blind or lacking in visual experience for any other reason.

Subthreshold Visualization

States of anxiety or depression are triggered by pertinent visual imagery which may be persistent or intermittent, clear or vague, steady or fleeting, observable or unobservable. If this pertinent visual imagery is persistently absent, from whatsoever cause, the anxiety or depression tends to diminish and to disappear.

An explanation of the term *unobservable* visual imagery is needed. If unobservable, obviously its existence becomes a matter of inference and assumption.

The argument for this assumption, more properly called a working hypothesis, is as follows: Action-potential measurements and the reports of our trained subjects in health and in disorder have agreed in their indication that ordinarily there is a state of continuing tension in the skeletal musculature of man and animals during ordinary rest. To this I have applied the term *residual tension,* which had been employed by Charles S. Sherrington in his observations on certain reflex states in animals.

Residual tension in the extraocular muscles is readily identified upon action-potential measurements during ordinary rest in man with eyelids closed. Subjective reports commonly agree with the objective data. The subjects often add that the tension is related to directing or focussing the eyes in order to see objects in imagination. With progressive relaxation of residual ocular tension, they report progressive diminution of visualization.

In the course thereof a stage is reached where tension is slight but the trained subject is in doubt whether he is still visualizing slightly. We assume that the visualization now exceeds the lower limits of observation. If the subject observes it, his ocular muscles become more active.

Accordingly, it seems reasonable to assume that just as the size of a seen object can be diminished until it passes beyond the lower limits of visual discrimination, likewise visual imagery can become so diminished as to pass beyond the threshold of identification even by the most highly trained observer. I shall call such hypothetical experience "subvisualization." I assume that it is conscious but imperceptible. I am inclined to believe that subvisualization is a missing link in the psychology of imagery.[6]

Selective Relaxation

From a practising standpoint in medicine or neuropsychiatry, our task becomes to teach the patient to attain a greater degree and length of maintenance of general eye relaxation upon lying-

---

[6] Psychologists will recall that Stout (1896) was among the first to maintain the occurrence in consciousness of "imageless thought." "There is no absurdity," Titchener quotes him in stating, "in supposing a mode of presentational consciousness which is not composed of visual, auditory, tactual and other experiences derived from and in some degree resembling in quality the sensations of the special senses." In the language of today (1966) we should reply to Stout that our interest centers on the positive evidence, if any, for the "presentational consciousness" he speaks of. If he presents no evidence, and he does not, we shall not feel that he has made a case for "imageless thought."

James Angell is quoted by Titchener in refutation of Stout. Angell finds in his own experience "a matrix of vague, shifting, auditory word images—accompanied by a tingling sense of irradiating meaning." Stout counters that this "tingling sense" is precisely what he calls "imageless apprehension." Thus they become lost in a battle of words. We can clear up the smoke under the assumption that both contestants might have been satisfied if they had known of evidence for subvisualization and other forms of (perceptually) subthreshold conscious imagination.

What we here discuss, as Titchener pointed out, are also precisely the sort of thing which German investigators had designated as "Bewusstseinslage." TITCHENER, E. B.: *Experimental Psychology of the Thought Processes*, New York, Macmillan, 1909, pp. 98-101; STOUT, O. O.: *Anal. Psychol.*, i:85; ANGELL, J. R.: Thought and Imagery. *Philos, Rev., vi*: 648, 1897, *ibid.,* 534.

down practice, but also upon sitting practice, with lids open as well as with lids closed. Furthermore, the patient is to be taught to discriminate visual imagery which pertains to his difficulties from that which pertains to other matters of his daily life and of his reflections. Having achieved such discrimination, he can learn to relax selectively that imagery which pertains to his troubles. He engages in repetition toward making this a habit. When such practice becomes automatic, he becomes more free to engage in his ordinary duties and pursuits of the day, for he is no longer distracted from them by his continual anxiety patterns of tensions and imagery. Physiologically restated, the latter tend to inhibit the tension patterns and images associated with and necessary to healthy pursuits. Accordingly, when anxiety tension no longer interferes, the patient returns to his healthy patterns. Gradually the patient passes into normality.

Occupational therapy for anxiety is the attempt to distract. Since thus it lessens the anxiety by inhibition, it is not surprising that frequently it not only fails but leads the patient into greater emotional disturbance. He makes efforts to forget his troubles and his tensions mount often to the breaking point, thanks to the well-intentioned occupational therapy. In my own practice the patient is not given occupational therapy. He is not driven into pursuits chosen by others for him, but is allowed to select for himself. If he chooses to continue at his daily duties, this is strongly recommended.

The Technique Proves Rewarding

To the practitioner who is a novice to such discriminations, the technique required may seem hair-splitting or otherwise recondite. Let me assure him that the anxious or depressed patient is interested in his condition. Accordingly a good teacher can build on this interest. As for the subject being highly technical, if this should so appear to some, my answer is that running an airplane also is technical and must be learned by steps. Science is that way, whether we like it or not, and so is the application of science in any form of engineering, including the self-engineering of man. To make such application appear less abstruse and more attainable, more preparation is required in basic sciences. I hope that doctors in all fields, including neuropsychiatrists, will come to realize that when they have selected for their study the most complex of fields known to man, namely, man himself, they have a self-imposed obligation to become skilled in more of the basic sciences than would be required in a less complex field of study such as mathematics, physics or chemistry.

SUMMARY ON EMOTION, INCLUDING NEW PRINCIPLES

In recent decades, the anatomy of emotion has taken on a new look. To the fore has come the limbic lobe, hitherto neglected! We can be most thankful to the intensified interest of numerous contributors, particularly in the realm of animal research.

Perhaps, in consequence, the time is ripe when we can add flesh to the skeleton of our knowledge. It would appear that to some extent what has been uncovered is emotion disembodied. Our present thesis is that emotion is as emotion does and our interest centers in intact man. Accordingly, we find functions in emotion which in the past have been overlooked. In the following we include old as well as new light on emotion.

1. Emotion is a generic term applied to various different momentary or prolonged reactions with a common characteristic, namely, excitation of vegetative nervous system responses.

2. Every emotional state differs from person to person and in the same person from moment to moment. Often the emotion has a developmental phase, proceeds to climax with some duration of plateau and then subsides.

3. Every emotional state has function of appropriate responsiveness to the reality of the moment.

4. The emotion is part of a manner of perception, part of an act of evaluation, part of an act of motor response.

5. Perception is colored differently, so to speak, in each type of emotional state, including anxiety, anger, love and others. (Different types of emotion are not to be sharply differentiated from each other. The class distinctions are derived from general experience of mankind and need not be defined scientifically. We know what we mean in a general way.)

6. Evaluation is found to be a visceral function, although not exclusively.

7. Striated neuromuscular action is coincident with perception and evaluation and takes part in these functions, rather than (as commonly conceived) merely the final common path perform- ance.

8. The brain in many respects is comparable with "Central" of the telephone system. Accordingly, brain centers in emotion (as in thinking) act *concurrently* with the peripheral emotive processes, not prior to them.

9. Imagery, with attendant tensions, often triggers the emo- tional state.

10. Probably the imagery in normal man always includes visual pictures, however faint and evanescent in some.

11. The physiology of emotion is based in part upon residual neuromuscular tension and

12. Probably on subvisualization and other imagery below threshold of autosensory observation, being too faint, too fast and too fleeting.

13. When emotion appears and develops, perception and eval- uation are modified according to the type of the emotion. Anx- iety, for example, brings perception and evaluation different from anger or joy. Reasoning is changed accordingly. (We speak of wishful thinking. We can speak quite as significantly of other emotional varieties of thinking, including angry thinking, joyous thinking and anxious thinking, illustrated often in the foregoing case studies. Likewise we can speak of action modified by emo- tion, to wit, angry action, joyous action, anxious action and a host of other types.)

14. Most neglected for the understanding of emotion and in- dispensible for control is the role of the striated musculature in perception and evaluation as well as in motor response. What is forgotten is that striated muscle tissue is the *only road to choice in the life of man and higher animals.* Here is the anatomical locus of all possible freedom of effort—at the disposal of the organism. I have emphasized that insofar as striated muscle ac- tion enters into the physiology of emotion, emotion is not exclu-

sively passive and involuntary; on the contrary, a voluntary element engages in every emotion which the doctor or the psychologist can not afford to ignore. Never are we *wholly driven* by emotion, although often it may so appear!

Nevertheless, the voluntary element in emotion should not be exaggerated. Emotion is largely passive, although partly voluntary. As for possible control, it would be folly to expect 100 per cent achievement by any method whatsoever, now or in the future. Conservatively, we may employ a simile: Bronze is made of copper and tin. Accordingly, to prevent the manufacture of bronze, it would suffice to withhold all tin. Similarly, to control emotion at any moment, as we have shown, it will suffice to maintain the specifically involved striated neuromusculature at approximately zero levels. To diminish emotion it will serve to relax the specifically involved striated neuromusculature partially.[7]

---

[7] It is important to remember that emotion will not diminish proportionally with tension. The mathematical relationship can not yet be stated, but it clearly is not $E=kt$, where E stands for emotion, k for a constant and t for striated neuromuscular tension.

Chapter X

THE PHYSIOLOGICAL BASIS OF
NEUROMUSCULAR RELAXATION
ACCORDING TO GELLHORN

Emotion and Other Mental Activities

ＩN THE preceding chapter evidence from the present investigations on man was outlined indicating that when neuromuscular relaxation advances, emotional states and other mental activities subside.[1] Presumably this signifies that both neocortical and limbic lobe-hypothalamic activity show parallel changes upon progressive neuromuscular relaxation. As said previously, these changes become especially notable when the tension pattern microvoltages fall in the neighborhood of zero levels.

Gellhorn Repeats Our Studies

E. Gellhorn has subjected these findings in man to parallel studies on laboratory animals. In view of the skill, ingenuity and thoroughness of this master physiologist, he has performed a crucial experiment for which neuropsychiatrists can be grateful. His investigations will be outlined in this chapter, but every reader is urged to refer to the original reports.[2]

To Relax He Curarizes

Gellhorn reminds us that proprioceptive impulses elicited in the muscles and joints by passive movements of the limbs cause

---

[1] However, they do not subside in proportion. It is not found that $E_m = kTe$, where E_m represents an emotional state, Te magnitude of muscular tension pattern in action-potentials and k a constant. The mathematical relationship remains to be determined.

[2] GELLHORN, E.: The influence of curare on hypothalamic excitability and the electroencephalogram. *Electroenceph. Clin. Neurophysiol.*, 10:697-703, Nov., 1958; The physiological basis of neuromuscular relaxation. *Arch. Intern. Med. (Chicago)*, 102: 392-399, Sept., 1958.

a marked excitation of the sympathetic division of the hypothalamus and a diffuse excitation of the cerebral cortex.[3] Reduction in hypothalamic excitability by barbiturates or by hypothalamic lesions[4] diminish or abolish the diffuse hypothalamic cortical discharge, whereas opposite results follow inhalation of 10 per cent CO_2. These observations suggested to Gellhorn that the reduction or abolition of proprioceptive impulses by curarization should diminish hypothalamic excitability and thus should diminish discharges from the hypothalamus to the cortex, whereupon synchrony should increase in the EEG.

Electrodes in Sympathetic Division of Hypothalamus

Accordingly, records of potentials from the posterior hypothalamus (sympathetic division) were made in twelve lightly anesthetized cats. Femoral arterial blood pressure was recorded and also reaction of the nictitating membrane with normal and with denervated preparations. These peripheral responses served as tests of sympathetic nerve activity.

Gellhorn tested the action of substances which produce neuromuscular relaxation because, like curare, they paralyze efferent nerve end-plate terminals in muscles. For brief curare-like action he injected intramuscularly purified chondodendron tomentosum extract (Intocostrin®); for brief action, succinylcholine (Anectine®). Before and after the injection he employed a square-wave generator to stimulate the sympathetic (posterior) section of the hypophysis. This sympathetic division of the hypophysis became less responsive, as indicated by diminished response of the nictitating membrane. The lessened response was shown to occur before any fall of blood pressure. Yet as neuromuscular relaxation progressed, under the influence of Intocostrin, both the contraction of the nictitating membrane and the pressor effect of pos-

---

[3] BERNHAUT, M., GELLHORN, E., and RASMUSSEN, A. T.: Experimental contributions to the problem of consciousness. *J. Neurophysiol.*, 16:21-35, Jan., 1953.

[4] GELLHORN, E.: The hypothalamic-cortical system in barbiturate anesthesia. *Arch. Int. Pharmacodyn.*, 93:434-442, 1953; KOELLA, W. P., and GELLHORN, E.: The influence of diencephalic lesions upon the action of nociceptive impulses and hypercapnia on the electrical activity of the cat's brain. *J. Comp. Neurol.*, 100:243-255, 1954.

terior hypothalamic stimulation likewise declined progressively.[5]

Anectine acts like Intocostrin, but more transiently. Accordingly, the effects following intramuscular injection were alike with the two substances, except that the full diminution of posterior hypothalamic response persisted only about four minutes. Thus, the effect of Anectine was shown to be reversible.

Gellhorn showed that the response of the nictitating membrane depended upon the integrity of its efferent nerve supply. Posterior hypothalamic stimulation failed to elicit marked contraction when the membrane had been denervated.

In collaboration with associates he had shown that asphyxia increases sympathetic response, i.e., the nictitating membrane then shows increased contraction upon posterior hypothalamic stimulation. After curarization had produced neuromuscular relaxation, however, asphyxia no longer increased nictitating membrane contraction.

Neuromuscular Relaxation Lessens Hypothalamic Sympathetic Excitability

From the experiments recounted, Gellhorn concluded that neuromuscular relaxation (produced by curarization) lessens hypothalamic sympathetic excitability.

Lessens Cortical Excitability

Thereafter Gellhorn recorded action-potentials from electrodes in the left and right hypothalamus and in the left motor-parietal cortex and in the left and right motor cortex. Before curarization, grouped potentials, evidencing diminished brain activity (which characteristically appear during general relaxation and sleep), were absent. After Anectine curarization, grouped potentials appeared in both the hypothalamic and cortical records and they persisted for several minutes. Analysis showed that the low frequencies were increased in the hypothalamic records, as is characteristic in general relaxation and sleep. Longer persisting

---

[5] *Cf.* JACOBSON, E.: *Progressive Relaxation.* Chicago; U. of Chicago, 2nd ed., 1938.

effects of similar significance followed the injection of Intocostrin (except for a transient excitatory phase).

The results recounted above furnish evidence that upon neuro-muscular relaxation (produced by curarization) there ensues reduction of sympathetic hypothalamic responsiveness; the hypo-thalamus quiets down, so to speak, showing grouped potentials, because proprioceptive impulses from muscles are reduced.

Previously, Gellhorn and associates had shown that animal responses to nociceptive stimulation depends upon hypothalamic excitability.[6] Gellhorn reports that in cats under light anesthesia, signs of relaxation in the form of grouped potentials in the hypo-thalamus and in the neocortex disappeared upon weak nocicep-tive stimulation, but largely returned following curarization.

Thus Gellhorn finds that neuromuscular relaxation produced by curarization diminishes response and excitation in the sympa-thetic division of the hypothalamus. Reduction in hypothalamic excitability explains also the lessened effect of nociceptive stimuli on the cerebral cortex and on the hypothalamus.

Muscle Tone Contributes to Hypothalamic and Cortical Excitation

These effects, he states, apparently result from the elimination of proprioceptive impulses (from muscle and joints) during neuromuscular relaxation produced by curarization. The effects of curare, he continues, "suggest that the physiological muscle tone contributes to hypothalamic and cortical excitation. The frequently observed occurrence of increased muscle tension in states of emotion seems to be not only the result of increased central sympathetic and somatic discharges whose parallelism at the hypothalamic level was emphasized by Hess (1947)[7] but also to the secondary contribution of the increased proprioceptive impulses to the state of excitation of the sympathetic division of the hypothalamus and of the cerebral cortex."

---

[6] BERNHAUT, GELLHORN, and RASMUSSEN, loc. cit.
[7] HESS, W. R.: Vegetative Funktionen und Zwischenhirn. Basel, 1947.

Gellhorn's Conclusion About Relaxation

These findings lead Gellhorn to the following conclusion: "*The value of a therapy of muscular relaxation (Jacobson 1929)*[8] *appears, therefore, well founded physiologically in states of emotional tension, regardless of the mechanism by which this relaxation is achieved.*"[9]

Gellhorn's Further Studies

In his investigation, entitled *The Physiological Basis of Neuromuscular Relaxation*, Gellhorn tests once more whether the findings of Jacobson during neuromuscular relaxation in man apply likewise to laboratory animals.

The apparent parallelism between the state of excitability of the hypothalamus and emotional reactivity, he notes, makes an investigation of the factors determining hypothalamic excitability a matter of importance for clinical medicine and neuropsychiatry.[10]

How can hypothalamic excitability be lowered? Gellhorn recalls that increased blood pressure in the isolated carotid sinus in the unanesthetized dog induced muscular relaxation and even sleep, whereas lowered pressure in the same region increased

---

[8] JACOBSON, E.: *Progressive Relaxation.* Chicago, U. of Chicago, 1st ed., 1929.

[9] GELLHORN, E.: *Electroenceph. Clin. Neurophysiol.*, 10:701, Nov., 1958.

[10] The fundamental role of the sympathetic division of the hypothalamus, he notes, has been established in classical investigations (BARD, P.: A diencephalic mechanism for the expression of rage with special reference to the nervous system. *Amer. J. Physiol.*, 84:490, 1928; RANSON, S. W.: Some functions of the hypothalamus. Harvey Lecture. *Bull N.Y. Acad. Med.*, 13:241, 1931; HESS, W. R., *loc. cit.*). Recent work, he adds, shows that emotional reactions may be evoked by stimulation and ablation of rhinencephalic structures, which suggests that hypothalamic excitability and emotional reactivity depend also on interrelations between the hypothalamus and the cortex (MURPHY, J. P., and GELLHORN, E.: Influence of hypothalamic stimulation on cortically induced movements and on action potentials of the cortex. *J. Neurophysiol.*, 8:341, 1945; Further investigations on diencephalic-cortical relations and their significance for the problem of emotion. *J. Neurophysiol.*, 8:431, 1945). The central role of the hypothalamus in emotion, he continues, is not altered by the finding that impulses from the reticular formation are necessary for the maintenance of hypothalamic excitability and wakefulness (GELLHORN, E.: *Autonomic Imbalance and the Hypothalamus.* Minneapolis, U. of Minn., 1957).

neuromuscular excitability. The relaxation effect (including diminished knee jerk) is attributable to increased parasympathetic discharges of the baroreceptors of the sinus with reciprocally diminished sympathetic discharges.[11]

When sympathetic excitability is lowered, somatic nervous excitability is lowered also. Gellhorn reminds us that lesions in the sympathetic section of the hypothalamus lead to loss of muscle tone and to somnolence.[12]

Protoveratrine intravenous injections increase the parasympathetic (baroreceptor) discharges from the carotid sinus. Thereupon blood pressure falls; no longer, however, after the sinoaortic area is denervated. Heymans and others had shown that baroreceptor discharges affect the medulla.[13] Gellhorn tested whether the baroreceptor discharges act also on the sympathetic division of the hypothalamus. He used cats: (a) normals; (b) others in which minute quantities of barbiturates has been injected bilaterally close to the mamillary bodies, lowering excitability of the sympathetic division of the hypothalamus; and (c) others in which a portion of this division had been destroyed by high frequency coagulation.

Protoveratine injection produced a fall of 37 mmHg in eleven normal cats, but only 5.9 mmHg in the others. After the barbiturate effect had been allowed to wear off, the cats in the second group reacted like the normals. Since protoveratine fails to produce hypotension in sympathectomized animals, Gellhorn assumes that protoveratine has an inhibiting action on the sympathetic system. His findings indicate, accordingly, that inhibition of the sympathetic division of the hypothalamus plays a decisive role in carotid sinus reflexes.

Baroceptor discharges increase when blood pressure is elevated upon injection of arterenol and epinephrine. Gellhorn recorded nictitating membrane contraction, blood pressure and heart rate

---

[11] Koch, E.: Die Irradiation der Pressoreceptorischen Kreislaufreflexe. *Klin. Wschr.*, 11:225, 1932.

[12] Ranson, S. W.: Somnolence caused by hypothalamic lesions in the monkey. *Arch. Neurol. and Psychiat. (Chicago)*, 41:1, 1939.

[13] Heymans, C., Bouckaert, J. J., and Regniers, P.: *Le Sinus Carotidien*. Paris, Gaston Doin & Cie, 1933.

in lightly anesthetized cats. He stimulated electrically the sympathetic division of the hypothalamus, measuring excitability thereof in terms of nictitating membrane response. Arterenol decreased this excitability. However, no such decrease was effected if the sinoaortic area had been denervated, thus eliminating the sinoaortic baroreceptors.

Gellhorn's findings indicated, then, that rise in sinoaortic pressure induced by arterenol leads—via baroreceptor reflexes—to lessened excitability of the sympathetic division of the hypothalamus. But his previous researches, as indicated on preceding pages, had shown that lessened excitability in the sympathetic division of the hypothalamus diminishes hypothalamic discharges to the cortex whereby cortical action-potentials increase in sleep-like groups. In contrast, if excitatory drugs are injected in this division, sleep-like groupings in a cat anesthetized with a barbiturate are reduced. Accordingly, he anticipated that action-potential signs of cortical excitability would be reduced following injection of arterenol. He found this to be true. The amplitude of the potentials at low frequencies was increased and at high frequencies decreased. After sinoaortic denervation the effect of arterenol generally was reversed.

Thus, Gellhorn found additional evidence that in normal cats the sympathetic division of the hypothalamus discharges into the cortex and thereby increases cortical excitability.

That proprioceptive impulses from muscles are powerful activators of the sympathetic division of the hypothalamus had been shown.[14] Their action appears in changes in the hypothalamogram, indicating excitation, and also in diffuse excitatory changes in the cerebral cortex resulting from increased discharges from the hypothalamus. "These findings suggest that a relaxation of the skeletal musculature is accompanied by a diminution in the state of excitability of the sympathetic division of the hypothalamus and, through a reduction in the hypothalamic-cortical discharges, by a similar reduction in the state of excitability of the cerebral cortex."

To produce neuromuscular relaxation in this study, Gellhorn

---

[14] BERNHAUT, GELLHORN, and RASMUSSEN, *loc. cit.*

once more curarized cats with Intocostrin and Anectine. Following the injection of Anectine, sympathetic response to electrical
stimulation was found to be greatly reduced in the hypothalamus,
as indicated by lessened contraction of the sympathetically innervated nictitating membrane. The effect is completely reversed
after the drug influence wears off. This reversibility is independent of blood pressure, which changes progressively. Reduced
sympathetic response of the hypothalamus to electrical stimulation was noted also following injection of chondodendron tomentosum extract, as shown by lessened pressor effect and lessened
acceleration of the heart rate.

Previously, it had been shown in Gellhorn's laboratory that
changes in the excitability of the sympathetic division of the
hypothalamus are accompanied by parallel changes in the intensity of discharges from the hypothalamus to the cortex. Following injection of Intocostrin or Anectine, independently of blood
pressure change, the cortex was reduced in excitability, since
large grouped potentials appeared in various cortical areas (like
those which follow injection of barbiturates either intravenously
or into the sympathetic section of the hypothalamus).

What is the effect of neuromuscular relaxation on the behavior
of unanesthetized cats? To answer this question, Gellhorn implanted electrodes into the lateral hypothalamic region and applied a stimulating current. Thereupon, neuromuscular relaxation
produced by curarization diminished the nicitating membrane
(sympathetic) response. This result was in accord with the fact
that the sympathetic division of the hypothalamus is demonstra-
bly involved in the emotional process and furnished additional
evidence that neuromuscular relaxation is likewise involved.

Muscle Relaxation Quiets Hypothalamus (Sympathetic Division) and also Cerebral Cortex

Thus, Gellhorn showed that the sympathetic division of the
hypothalamus and also the cortex are quieted when proprioceptive impulses from muscles diminish, since it is shown that these
impulses contribute importantly to the excitability of the hypothalamus, and also (via upward discharges from the hypothalamus) to the state of cortical excitation.

The results of his manifold investigations lead Gellhorn to state as follows: "The applicability of these findings to human physiology and pathology rests on physiological and clinical observations in man:

1. The extensive work of Jacobson who emphasizes the occurrence of muscle tension evidenced by the electromyogram . . . in emotional states.[15] His clinical observations lead him to the conclusion that 'emotions subside as the individual *completely* relaxes the striated muscles.' Moreover he finds that muscular relaxation diminishes mental activities."

Findings Confirmed

Thus in his extensive investigations on laboratory animals (cats), Gellhorn sees confirmation of my findings in man: that with advancing neuromuscular relaxation, and the accompanying decrease of proprioceptive sensations from muscles, emotion and other mental activity subside.

Gellhorn adds that the applicability of his findings to human physiology and pathology bears also on "2. Kleitman's (1939) observation that prolonged wakefulness depends on priorioceptive impulses. As soon as the experimental subjects under such conditions were permitted to lie down they fell asleep."[16]

These observations, as Kleitman knew (and often related to his classes), confirmed my earlier observations that sleep sets in upon diminution of priorioceptive impulses. As early as 1908 to 1911, I reported that proprioceptive sensations diminish upon neuromuscular relaxation until sleep ensues.[17] The reduction of proprioceptive impulses is the key to the method of progressive relaxation applied to insomnia. In 1917, I began to apply this clinically to the treatment of insomnia and other states of undue

---

[15] Gellhorn mentions also two other references, namely: SMITH, A. A.: An electromyographic study of tension in interrupted and completed tasks. *J. Exp. Psychol.,* 46:32, 1953; NEWMAN, P. P.: Electromyographic studies of emotional states in normal subjects. *J. Neurol. Neurosurg. Psychiat.,* 16:200, 1953.

[16] KLEITMAN, N.: *Sleep and Wakefulness.* Chicago, U. of Chicago, 1939.

[17] JACOBSON, E.: *Inhibition.* Doctorate thesis, Cambridge, Harvard, 1910; Further experiments on the inhibition of sensations. *Amer. J. Psychol.,* XXIII: 345-369, July, 1912.

tension and soon thereafter reported thereon in medical journals.[18] Decades later, Kleitman became interested in my findings
and lectured yearly on them to his classes, as his students related;
these findings showed the relationship of relaxation to sleep, as
I had suggested. His findings on subjects who were artificially
kept awake for days supported further my relaxation theory of
sleep. So far as I know, Kleitman never claimed that he origi-
nated the relaxation theory of sleep, namely, that sleep ensues
upon the diminution of proprioceptive sensations from muscles.
Occasionally he referred an insomniac for treatment here.

To this I can add that, under controlled conditions, when
microvoltage levels of striated muscles are persistent over periods
of approximately thirty seconds or more, particularly including
eye and speech musculature, emotion and other mental activity
subside to the point of normal sleep. Thus, diminution of proprioceptive sensations is shown to be important both scientifically
and clinically. Accordingly, since 1917, I have employed progressive relaxation methodology in clinical practice in cases of
insomnia as well as of anxiety and other forms of neurosis.

---

[18] JACOBSON, E.: Use of relaxation in hypertensive states. *New York Med. J.*,
March 6, 1920, p. 2; Treatment of nervous irritability and excitement. *Illinois Med.
J.*, Mar., 1921, p. 1; Reduction of nervous irritability and excitement by progressive
relaxation. *Transactions, Section on Nervous and Mental Diseases.* 1920, p. 5.

Most important for sleep is diminution of *kinesthetic* sensations, particularly
those from muscles. By blockage of passage of impulses at muscular end-plates,
curarization diminishes afferent impulses.

Chapter XI

CLINICAL EXPERIENCE WITH EMOTIONS
AND METHODS OF CONTROL

Every doctor has the opportunity for vast experience on the emotions of man. In large part his success as a practitioner depends upon his knowledge of, and his reactions to the emotional states of his patients. This experience and knowledge, I dare say, is no less important than that gained by laboratory experimenters on the emotions of animals. However, the latter has the advantage of being scientific. Accordingly, conclusions can be drawn of general significance and their degree of probability can be estimated, which is more than can be said of the daily experience of the doctor with emotional patients.

We can ask: What specialty offers best preparation for the doctor for effective practice on his emotional patients? Since it is often estimated that at least 50 per cent of the symptoms of patients derive from or are largely induced by their emotional states, this question is important. Shall the general practitioner refer his emotional patients to the psychiatrist, whose interest in emotion is recognized? In answering this question, we shall need to take into account the principles outlined in the present volume. According to these principles, emotion can no longer be regarded as something occurring exclusively or chiefly in the brain or so-called mind, but instead involves active participation of every system of the entire organism. When emotional patients show symptoms of constipation or diarrhea, when their symptoms indicate the presence of spastic esophagus, when they begin to show signs of peptic ulcer, when their blood pressure becomes elevated, when oppression in the chest or distress in the left arm or elsewhere elicits suspicion of coronary insufficiency, when lowered basal metabolism together with lowered values of blood pressure or other signs point to the presence of chronic fatigue, when these and other common signs of tension disorder appear in emotional patients, the general practitioner or the internist may be interested in these manifestations of emotion even more than the psychiatrist. For the symptoms and signs of tension disorder manifesting themselves in the cardiovascular or the digestive system or in the general resistance of the patient to various infections and other diseases have up to the present been regarded as belonging more to the general practitioner and the internist than to the psychiatrist.

Clinical laboratory tests in systemic disorders other than those of the nervous system likewise are more familiar to the general practitioner and to the internist. We all appreciate that in past decades the introduction of clinical laboratory tests has tended to render our daily medical practice more scientific. Furthermore, I would here suggest that the introduction of action-potential measurements can add much to the scientific character of the daily practice of medicine. In my opinion, graphs of action-potentials are no less important than graphs of blood pressure, temperature, respiration and other clinical variables now regarded as standard. I believe that the doctor will never understand his patient until he recognizes the tension disorders clearly.

Tension disorders can be recognized scientifically when action-potentials are measured and graphed through the use of the integrating neurovoltmeter. I have described this sufficiently in past papers. It is necessary here to repeat that, for this purpose, commercial electromyographs are not sufficiently sensitive nor stable for use in medical offices and in hospitals. I need to emphasize also that commercial instruments used in electroencephalography are likewise inadequate to measure nervousness and to record emotional states. For measurements of neuromuscular patterns identifying tension disorders, it is necessary to have stable apparatus capable of accurate measurements down to a small fraction of a microvolt. On the whole, in this field our instruments are more advanced than those commonly used in electrocardiography. I am proud to say this.

Since our patients continually engage in emotion and other forms of mental activity, doctors and educators really need to understand the basic physiology of emotion and of other forms of mental activity. I have attempted to outline this in the present and in foregoing publications. Among other matters, I have stressed the basic character of neuromuscular contractions otherwise known as *tensions* and as *efforts*. Once their role is fully recognized, it becomes obvious that talking to our patients is not basic treatment. If we really aim to diminish their tension disorders or to influence them to a greater extent than can be accomplished by the use of sedatives and tranquilizers, by distraction, hobbies, vacations and occupational therapy, we must do more than counsel with our patients. No one ever learns to swim through conversation alone. It is not confidence that sustains the swimmer. Instead, it is the movement of his arms and legs. With proper movements of his limbs, he will swim, regardless of the presence or absence of confidence. To an important extent, I have found that the same provision applies in meeting the emotional states of our patients, including those in tension disorders. Accordingly, in medical practice on emotional patients, I advocate the use of sedatives and tranquilizers only as a crutch and the use of suggestion, autosuggestion and hypnosis approximately never. Reassurance is to be employed warily, if at all.

If the principles presented in this volume and in foregoing ones are sound, there is no merit in understatement of therapeutic results in the interest of conservatism. We scientists have inherited a tradition of understatement as marking the care and caution of our profession. It is in pleasing contrast with the blatant claims of advertisers of commercial and medical products over television, radio and newspapers. It is in pleasing contrast also with the obvious dishonesty of various claims of healers commonly labeled quackery. However, in the higher sciences of mathematics, of physics and of chemistry, writers do not practice understatement.

If the therapeutic aspects of the present investigations have been sufficiently controlled, as I believe, it would not be in the interest of science or of the public service to understate the results. In my opinion and experience, which includes the use of all other standard methods of approach to tension states and tension disorders, the physiological approach which has been employed is not only simple, clear and reproducable, but basic. This is to say that, according to my experience and understanding of the welfare response of human beings, methods of progressive relaxation and of self-operations control are specific. Their application is to a broad field of human maladies and educational needs, but, where indicated, these methods are as specific as is proper teaching in any other field of human education. We recognize that the use of antibiotics in human infection has introduced a new epoch into the practice of medicine in this field. The range and the specificity of antibiotics is under further investigation and further improvements in our knowledge and methods appears from time to time in the current literature. My thesis is that, in tension disorders, methods of physiological teaching can likewise be improved by careful investigation, but that in their general nature as applied to tension disorders and to what commonly are regarded as functional nervous states, these methods are specific.

Applying these physiological methods in the field of emotion common in every therapeutic practice, one of the most general forms is chronic or acute anxiety. It is no wonder that the doctor often sees anxious patients, because it is concern that brings them to the doctor's office. Sometimes he finds the concern objectively unwarranted, and he may tell the patient so. Nevertheless, a tendency to anxiety very often persists. Many patients, going from office to office, from doctor to doctor, are excessively self-involved. They bask on reassurance, but the effects are not long enduring. Anxiety-prone, they soon find something else of concern. Doctors themselves are not commonly free from anxiety. Many are concerned about their own pace of living, fearing that it may result in coronary disease. There is no need to remind the reader that life abounds with difficulties which may incite anxiety tensions.

Accordingly, we turn to the consideration of our clinical experience since 1920 with patients suffering from anxiety states and other forms of excessive emotion *insofar as this relates to biology of human emotions.* We can ask, do our principles, when applied practically, produce favorable medical and psychological results? This can be regarded as a therapeutic test of the soundness of our principles.

In the interests of public service, this question should be answered with neither overstatement nor understatement. I can answer only from my own clinical experience with methods of tension control as compared with other methods. I have used approximately all standard methods of psychotherapy, as well as a vast array of pharmaceuticals. My answer also is based upon results I have seen from the use of other methods by other doctors. From these points of view, in my experience, the use of methods of physiological tension control affords a considerable advance.

These methods take into account and treat directly not only the psychiatric aspect of anxiety and other emotion but likewise the inevitable accompanying pathophysiology of the organs of the gastrointestinal tract, the cardiovascular tract and other systems. Accordingly, they constitute an approach to the whole patient which has hitherto been lacking both in psychiatry and in internal medicine and even in general practice.

Furthermore, upon applying tension-control methods, the therapeutic results can be estimated by scientific and statistical measures. Our action-potential measurements show that clinical improvement in the hyperemotional patient generally is marked by lowered values. There occurs concommitant improvement in the gastrointestinal, cardiovascular and organic symptoms. Needless to say, improvement does not occur continuously. By no means do we find that "every day and in every way the patient becomes better." This statement by a popular advocate of suggestive therapy does not apply. Instead, the patients are dealt with realistically. In advance they are informed that the course of improvement never runs smooth but is marked by ups and downs. Often the relapses can be severe. Sometimes the relapse is so severe that the patient complains of being worse than when instruction was begun.

It is germane to add that, from the onset, the patient is instructed that nothing will be done for him by the doctor toward the lessening of tension disorder, except to afford him instruction. It is no different from his entering a course of instruction to drive a plane or a motor car, to learn engineering or any other scientific or practical art. The aim is independence and freedom from habits of wasteful tension and imagery. In plain terms, he is to be *on his own*—independently so. This applies clearly to hypo-chondriac emotion, which is so often seen in patients showing anxiety states.

We now consider cases previously published in a volume en-titled *Anxiety and Tension Control;* and in two other volumes, now approximately ready for publication, *Case Histories of Anx-iety* and *A Case of Anxiety Control.*

In Chart A on page 166, a total of twenty-five cases is pre-sented, selected from a larger list of cases with similar diagnoses, because these received a full or purposely abridged course of in-struction and could be reached after years for follow-up exami-nation or for other needed data.

As will be noted, there were nineteen males and six females, with twenty-four white and one Negro. Before instruction, the age range was from nineteen to sixty-six years. Suffering from emotions was severe and chronic in all cases. In many, disability was marked. Many had received psychoanalytic or other psycho-therapeutic treatment, often for years, with little or no improve-ment. Tranquilizers and sedatives had been employed with amelioration of symptoms temporarily only and many times with side-effects. One of the purposes of tension control instruction was to break the habit of seeking relief through medication, af-fording an independence in the patient previously lacking, espe-cially in the hypochondriac. This purpose was accomplished in twenty-four of twenty-five cases and confirmed in the follow-up. The exception will be discussed.

A large variety of unpleasant emotions appeared both from the complaints of the patients and as revealed by their behavior. Room in the column headed "Emotion" was not sufficient to list them all. Fears, phobias and depression appeared in many, and some were suicidal. Two feared that they might kill.

Dates of notation of first improvement are shown, but we must consider that improvement often begins without being recorded. The patient may be slow to note the change, which may be ob-served first by the doctor or by a member of the family or may be revealed upon electrical recording of considerably reduced action-potentials. The significance of dates of first notation of improvement is further reduced because relapses commonly follow. Thereupon both the patient and the family may become discouraged over the results of treatment.

The proof, however, is shown in the last three columns. As will be seen, at the close of instruction the patients typically had become approximately free from all the original emotional symptoms. This was their report, and the doctor agreed. Reduction of action-potentials was typical, where electrical recording was made.

In pleasing contrast with the severe concern I often experienced during the instruction of these patients, I am most impressed with the follow-up. As will be seen, the period of reported emotional improvement ranged up to forty years. Generally, the improvement proved lasting. This was most marked in those who maintained technical practice periods (not merely rest periods) daily or approximately so.

The exception to our effective results deserves comment. At the close of an abridged course in self-operations control, consisting of one hour of instruction at twenty-eight-day intervals, but with daily practice for about one year, the patient's emotional state was vastly improved. No longer was it necessary for her husband to remove razor blades and knives from their home, for fear that she might slit the throats of her four children. Homicidal and other fears and phobias appeared no longer. She had become cheerful and hopeful.

This benign state persisted for a year after discharge when, unfortunately and without letting me know, her husband secured a full-time position for her, disregarding her full-time duties with four small children and disregarding the adage "Let well enough alone." After two weeks of working she returned to the use of tranquilizers, from which she had been weaned. From this time on her emotional state relapsed. She continued with her dual occupation for an entire year, at the end of which I was notified and the patient came to Chicago to be under my care for several days. It proved to be too late. She slit her wrists. Although the injury was slight, depression set in severely. Neither anti-depressive medication nor reminders of tension control methods availed. The patient returned to New York in severe relapse and remained so.

CHART

Case	Diagnosis	Sex	Age	Color	Emotion
1	tension disorder sweating syndrome colitis barbiturate addiction	M	28	W	anxiety
2	obstructive duodenal ulcer tension disorder anxiety—chronic severe healed pulmonary tuberculosis	M	42	W	anxiety fears
3	tension disorder severe sweating syndrome spastic colon	M	22	W	anxiety depression at times embarrassment
4	postcoronary infarction insomnia severe fatigue	M	66	W	discouragement anxiety depression lack of interests
5	essential hypertension allergic reaction anxiety state insomnia prostatitis	M	54	W	anxiety (worried)
6	tension disorder spastic colon chronic insomnia chronic fatigue chronic prostatitis lumbosacral disc syndrome pyriformis syndrome	M	57	W	anxiety suffering
7	insomnia fatigue spastic colon	M	53	W	mild anxiety tension to drive
8	tension disorder hypochondria anxiety state spastic alimentary tract	M	61	W	anxiety easily shocked
9	anxiety tension, cardiac neurosis (persistent after psychoanalysis) and coronary insufficiency, chronic fatigue, spastic bowel	M	34	W	anxiety
10	anxiety with homicidal obsessive-compulsion nausea, weight loss, diarrhea	F	31	W	anxiety, phobias
11	phobic anxiety, dizziness, former nausea diagnosed as duodenal ulcer	F	28	N	anxiety

A

Instruction Date Begun—Date Ended		Improvement First Noted	Final Emotional State	Follow-up Date	Results
2 '56	9 '57	11 '56	healthy	1 '58	lasting
3 '56	11 '60	5 '56	healthy	3 '63	lasting
1 '51	1 '52	4 '51	healthy	3 '52	lasting
4 '59	5 '60	10 '59	healthy	12 '62	lasting
12 '57	3 '62	1 '58	healthy	10 '62	lasting
9 '57	3 '59	6 '58	healthy	10 '62	lasting
7 '60	11 '61	9 '60	anxiety-free	11 '62	lasting
4 '53	6 '55	4 '53	healthy (cheerful)	10 '62	much improved (pyrosis occasional)
10 '57	1 '60	12 '57	healthy	9 '62	lasting
4 '56	5 '57	4 '56	much worse	6 '60	severe relapse
8 '59	8 '60	10 '59	excellent	5 '61	healthy

CHART

Case	Diagnosis	Sex	Age	Color	Emotion
12	anxiety, psychoneurosis, chronic fatigue, spastic alimentary tract	F	49	W	anxiety
13	anxiety, phobias, periods of diarrhea (psychoneurotic anxiety tension)	F	34	W	anxiety
14	depression, chronic fatigue, anxiety	F	24	W	depression
15	anxiety, exhaustion, airophobia	M	32	W	anxiety
16	anxiety, phobias spastic alimentary tract (when nervous, belches sour fluid)	M	30	W	anxiety despondent
17	anxiety with compulsions constipation	M	37	W	phobias
18	anxiety and panic chronic fatigue constipation, diarrhea	M	40	W	hypochondria
19	anxiety with infanticidal obsession, compulsion, diarrhea, esophogospasm	F	30	W	anxiety, panic, depression
20	disabling anxiety diarrhea, gastric	M	41	W	anxiety, depression, hypochondria
21	anxiety persistent after psychoanalysis insomnia, nausea	M	33	W	phobias
22	anxiety tension, cardiac neurosis, coronary insuffi-ciency, phobias of travel (persistent after psychoanalysis) colic, diarrhea	M	33	W	phobias hypochondria depression
23	disabling anxiety insomnia, chronic fatigue	M	19	W	anxiety
24	sexual neurosis, chronic fatigue, insomnia, spastic colon	M	52	W	anxiety, jealousy
25	anxiety over organ inferiority	M	25	W	anxiety, shyness, feeling of inferiority

A (Continued)

Instruction Date Begun—Date Ended		Improvement First Noted	Final Emotional State	Follow-up Date	Results
10 '53	5 '55	10 '53	symptom-free	2 '60	lasting
12 '22	5 '24	1 '23	anxiety-free	5 '61	lasting
1 '34	11 '35	4 '34	anxiety-free	8 '60	lasting
10 '29	12 '31	11 '29	free of emotional disturbances	10 '60	lasting
6 '35	2 '39	7 '35	free from anxiety without relapse	6 '57	lasting
2 '36	12 '39	5 '36	free of anxiety	9 '60	lasting
12 '36	2 '42	1 '37	free of anxiety	7 '66	lasting
10 '41	12 '44	11 '41	approx. free of nerv. states; no fears, depression or compulsions	8 '65	lasting
5 '44	1 '54	6 '44	free of anxiety and depression	9 '66	lasting
6 '49	8 '49	6 '49	free of all original symptoms	12 '50	lasting
3 '49	3 '52	5 '49	free of all original symptoms	3 '61	lasting
5 '52	9 '60	5 '52	excellent, no relapse	7 '61	lasting
1 '56	2 '59	2 '56	free of all nervous and emotional symptoms	1 '61	lasting
5 '56	12 '58	6 '56	free of emotional difficulties	2 '61	lasting

The lesson for me was a forcible reminder of the necessity of keeping in touch with all patients after discharge, whenever possible.

We close this chapter, then, with the evidence favoring the use of tension control methods in cases of hyperemotionality with attendant symptoms of visceral disorder. As indicated, the results were markedly positive in twenty-four out of twenty-five cases.

We turn to examination of further evidence,—data secured even upon much briefer instruction, as related in the following chapter.

Chapter XII

ANXIETY IN U.S. NAVY AIR CADETS: GROUP INSTRUCTION

(As Reported by Commander William Neufeld, U.S.N.R.[1])

Anxiety states accompanied by fatigue, restlessness and insomnia, including what were called *breakdowns*, were reported by flight instructors at primary naval stations during the war days of 1943. While still making adjustment to Navy life and discipline, many cadets apparently failed to be sufficiently relaxed. States of excessive tension while learning to fly came to be recognized as a menace. At the same time, reports from combat zones indicated that one of the chief difficulties with which pilots had to contend was failure to relax. High nervous tension seemed to account for excessive loss of pilots and planes on first missions of combat duty.

To learn more about states of high nerve tension and fatigue at the Pre-Flight School, Chapel Hill, North Carolina, Drs. William L. Woods and Lucien Brouha of Harvard University observed cadets of the 23rd, 24th and 38th Battalions before and after a period of approximately eight weeks of ordinary preflight training. Many cadets reported a feeling of being tightened up. Others reported a period of tossing about before going to sleep.

---

[1] NEUFELD, WILLIAM: Relaxation methods in U.S. Navy Air Schools. *Amer. J. Psychiat.*, 108, 2:132-137, Aug., 1951. This article has been submitted to the Bureau of Medicine and Surgery, Department of the Navy, for official clearance, with the following endorsements: "Review of this material does not imply Department of Defense indorsement of factual accuracy or opinion" and also: "No objection to publication on grounds of military security. Office of Public Information, Department of Defense." (The letter stamp was dated 23 March 1951.) The opinions of assertions in this article are the private ones of the writer and are not to be construed as official or reflecting the views of the Navy Department or of the naval service at large. The present chapter is based on Commander Neufeld's published article and on other data which he forwarded to me.

Some appeared continually overactive or restless. Such symptoms often preceded or accompanied fatigue. The syndrome was designated *fatigue-tension*. The examiners employed a 4-point rating scale in recording their observations concerning fatigue-tension: 4—indicated no manifestation; 3—slight; 2—moderate; and 1—marked. Since the ratings shown in Table I merely summarize the clinical impression of the examiners regarding each cadet, no mathematical accuracy can be attributed to the figures. However, they are presented for their qualitative value.

The figures suggest that possibly somewhat less than half of the cadets showed moderate or marked manifestations of fatigue-tension.

Concerning subjective experiences at the five preflight schools, 3,181 cadets answered a written questionnaire. They had received at least eight weeks of regulation preflight training. To permit complete freedom, they were instructed not to sign their names. The questions were to be answered by *yes* or *no* or *excessive* or *moderate* or *none*. Because of limitations of space, I quote only eight of the twenty-two questions, including the results.

No quantitative value pertains to the results secured from any such questionnaire. However, the percentage as between the various five schools revealed a fair measure of agreement. We note the shortcomings of the questions, the subjective character of the answers, and the diverse interpretations of the same question doubtless made by different cadets. Nevertheless, some significance can be attached to the conclusion that most of the cadets reported nervous difficulties of one sort or another.

TABLE I

OCCURRENCE OF FATIGUE-TENSION

Fatigue-tension Rating	Number of Cases	Percentage
1	33	9.3
2	117	33.1
3	55	15.5
4	149	42.1
Total	354	100.0

QUESTIONNAIRE 1

		Replies	
Questions	Per cent	Yes	No

1. Upon retiring at night do you have trouble going to sleep?
   - Excessive — 5
   - Moderate — 31
   - None — 64
2. While in bed at night do you make frequent shifts or fidgets? — 39 — 61
3. After a night's sleep do you ever feel tired upon arising? — 76 — 24
4. Have you a tendency to worry about events of the next day? — 43 — 57
5. Previous to athletic contests have you ever become sick in the stomach? — 11 — 89
6. Do you ever worry about your own health? — 37 — 63
7. When you hear a sudden noise do you jump or feel startled? — 29 — 71
8. During periods of degrees of nervousness do tense feelings tend to make your mind confused? — 36 — 64

Averages of the 3,181 cadets having difficulties in each category gave the following results:

Sleep	48%	(4 questions)
Athletics	35%	(4 questions)
Worry, Anxiety	32%	(5 questions)
General	40%	(6 questions)

Training Course for Naval Officers to Become Instructors

Official arrangements were completed for five U.S. Naval Officers to come to the Laboratory for Clinical Physiology in Chicago to be trained as instructors. Each officer came from one of the chief preflight naval training schools in various states. The officers received daily training for five weeks. They formulated a training program for other officers with my approval and following their return to their respective schools in turn gave instruction to ninety-five other naval officers to be teachers. The one hundred officers thus trained in our emergency program trained about 15,300 cadets in the first eight months.

The course for the five officers in Chicago required approximately ten hours per day. Each officer was trained to relax three (nonsuccessive) hours per day in the lying or sitting posture. At the same time, principles and methods of teaching were stressed.

Progress was checked by electroneuromyometry. During some of the tests, additional instruction was given. Lectures were given on the physiology and psychology of states of fatigue, nervous irritability and excitement in their relationship to naval aviation training for combat. Psychosomatic problems that arose in the experience of the officers were discussed by all. Each officer practiced alone at least two hours per day. Since these men were accustomed to daily vigorous activities, at least one or two hours per day were devoted to athletic exercises.

Training Course for Cadets

As stated above, 15,300 cadets received relaxation training in the first eight months. Classes of cadets included up to three hundred members. The largest classes were supervised by about five officer-instructors. Because of many other required courses, the instruction was limited to three half-hour periods on three different days per week for twenty-six periods. It was admitted that the cadets did not practice one hour daily as desired.

The attempt was made to train the cadets to recognize their individual patterns of neuromuscular tension and to relax them when excessive.

Results of Relaxation Training: Comparisons with Control Groups

1. FATIGUE-TENSION SYNDROME. Cadets of one batallion were examined at Chapel Hill after their course of relaxation, and their ratings in fatigue-tension were determined in ten-minute personal interviews as compared with the ratings of two other batallions similarly determined but without relaxation training. As shown in Table II, the fatigue-tension syndrome was markedly dimin-

TABLE II

Ratings	Fatigue-Tension Number		Percentage	
	Group I No Relax	Group II Relax	Group I No Relax	Group II Relax
None	149	90	42.1	53.0
Slight	55	70	15.5	41.1
Moderate	117	10	33.1	5.9
Marked	33	0	9.3	0.0
	354	170	100.0	100.0

RELAXATION CHART

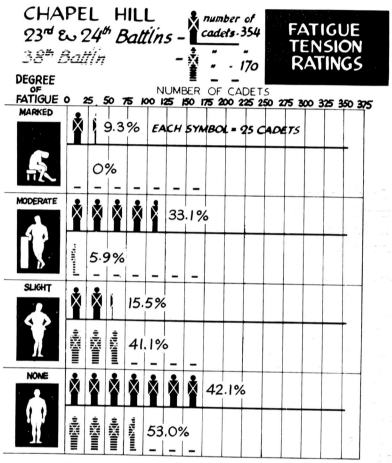

CHART I

ished in Group II cadets after relaxation training as compared with the untrained, control Group I (see also Chart I). After relaxation training, only 10 cadets out of 170 were rated as moderate in fatigue-tension, as compared with 117 out of 354 cadets who had no such training. In the untrained, thirty-three cadets were rated as exhibiting marked fatigue-tension, whereas none was so rated among those who had received the training.

TABLE III

INJURY REPORT FROM PREFLIGHT SCHOOL
IOWA CITY

	No Relaxation Training (238 Cadets)	Relaxation Training (983 Cadets)
Strains	24.	66.
Sprains	44.	137.
Dislocations	7.	11.
Fractures	6.	29.
Misc. (cuts, bruises, etc.)	6.	53.
Total injuries	87.	296.
Injuries per cadet	0.37	0.30
Per cent reduction		19.

Conclusions of the preflight instructors agreed with those of the Harvard investigators.

2. INJURIES AND ABSENTEEISM. Some influence of the relaxation training possibility can be inferred from the percentage of injuries and of resultant days of absence from physical training activities at preflight schools. Many of these activities were competive. Records from the Pre-Flight School at Iowa City concern four battalions, with a total of 1,221 cadets. The number of cadets used in control tests was far smaller than those who received relaxation training, making it difficult to draw conclusions with quantitative accuracy.[2]

Of the seventy days during which all cadets were scheduled for participation in physical training activities, the total number of injuries in the control group of 238 cadets was 87, while that in the battalions that received relaxation training (983) was 29.6. As shown in Table III the number of injuries per cadet was 0.37 in the control group, which fell to 0.30 in the test group, a reduction of about 19 per cent.

In the same groups (Table IV), the total number of days lost from injuries was 1.05 per cadet in the control group, but 0.65 in the group that received relaxating training, a reduction of 38 per cent.

---

[2] Report by Lt. Cdr. Fred Stalcup, Pre-Flight School, Iowa City, Iowa, 1944.

TABLE IV

REPORT OF DAYS LOST FROM INJURIES FROM
PREFLIGHT SCHOOL, IOWA CITY

	No Relaxation Training (238 Cadets)	Relaxation Training (983 Cadets)
Days lost from injuries	249.	635.
Days lost per cadet	1.05	0.65
Per cent reduction		38.

TABLE V

ATHLETIC ACHIEVEMENT OF CADETS WITH
AND WITHOUT RELAXATION TRAINING

	Initial Test		Final Test		Improvement	
	No Relax	Relax	No Relax	Relax	No Relax	Relax
Chins	7.93	8.16	9.73	9.70	1.80	1.54
Push-ups	24.47	25.32	28.87	29.60	4.40	4.28
Jump reach	21.84	21.94	22.39	22.37	0.55	0.43
Speed agility	32.66	32.53	31.64	31.18	—1.02	—1.35

3. ATHLETIC ACHIEVEMENT. The cadets of twelve battalions that had finished the brief course in relaxation training were compared with those of twelve other battalions without such training. In Table V the data are given from three of the preflight schools in which these cadets were stationed.

These figures show no marked differences between the test and control groups. However, it should be noted that the cadets who received relaxation training sacrificed one and one-half hours per week of time devoted by the cadets of the control group to practice in the conditioning program. Perhaps the only conclusion that can be safely drawn is that, notwithstanding the loss of time from physical training, the relaxation program did not retard the physical conditioning of the cadets.

Swimming grades of two battalions who had received relaxation training were compared with those of three other battalions under similar conditions, but without training to relax. On the average, the cadets with relaxation training passed 20 per cent more tests over a scheduled period than the cadets who did not have such training.[3]

---

[3] Report on swimming grades was furnished by Lt. Cdr. J. Smith, Officer in Charge of Swimming, Pre-Flight School at Del Monte, California.

4. SLEEP CHECK. A sleep check was carried out at three of the preflight schools.[4] At night, from taps to reveille, cadets were observed in their rooms, which were lit dimly. Each officer observed from four to eight cadets, keeping individual records.

The cadets, 340 in number, were observed in three preflight schools during their ninth week at these schools. Of these, 190 were without relaxation training while 140 were trained in twenty-six periods, each of thirty minutes.

Since observations were made under the same conditions, presumably the presence of officers and a low light in the room did not affect one group of cadets more than the other.

For each cadet the following items were recorded: (a) length of time from taps to apparent onset of sleep; (b) number of times and length of time awake during the night; (c) total loss of sleep in minutes; and (d) dreaming.

Hourly records were kept of full body turns; number of parts of body movements, e.g., moving leg, swinging arm, etc.; and talking or mumbling in sleep.

Some of the cadets who had no relaxation training made some surprisingly restless records. One cadet made forty-one body turns. Another moved parts of his body 132 times during the night. A third talked or mumbled sixteen times. At Del Monte, a cadet awoke six times during the night. Another cadet from the same school failed to sleep two hours and thirty-four minutes of the night. No such examples of severe restlessness were noted in the individuals who had received the training.

Results are summarized in Table VI.

Talking and mumbling were reduced to the greatest extent (56%). The number of times cadets awoke during the night was also reduced by over one-half (55%). The percentage of complete body turns and of shifts of parts of the body showed the least difference (27% and 28% respectively) (3).

Of the seven percentages shown in Table VI, each exceeds 25 per cent, and the average is approximately 38 per cent. The re-

---

[4] Sleep checks were made at preflight schools in Athens (Officer in Charge, Lt. Cdr. R. S. Warren), Del Monte (Officer in Charge, Lt. Cdr. Wm. Neufeld), and St. Marys (Officer in Charge, Lt. Cdr. F. M. Ingram), January 1944.

TABLE VI

SLEEP CHECK SUMMARY

COMBINED DATA FROM THREE PREFLIGHT SCHOOLS

Average for Cadet	No Relaxation (190 cadets)	Relaxation (140 cadets)	Difference %
Time from taps to sleep, in min.	22.7	15.4	32
Total loss of sleep, in min.	31.5	18.9	40
Number of times awake	.71	.32	55
Dreaming	.28	.20	29
Full body turns	12.0	8.8	27
Part body movements	31.2	22.4	28
Talking or mumbling	2.70	1.20	56

sults indicate that for the most part the cadets after relaxation training became able to go to sleep more quickly, were less restless during sleep hours, and lost less sleep.

During the last part of the night in cadets without relaxation training, bodily movements, including both full body turns and parts of body movements, were greatest. During the last two hours, cadets with relaxation training rested more quietly in respect to bodily movements.

In both groups, the period of greatest restlessness was between 0200 and 0300, including talking and mumbling. From the results it would seem that the most restful sleep occurred during the first two hours of sleep, which were before midnight. The results indicate that cadets who received relaxation training slept much more quietly (see also Charts II, III, IV, V).

5. CADET REACTION TO RELAXATION TRAINING. 3,238 cadets who had received relaxation training in four preflight schools wrote answers to a questionnaire omitting their names in order to insure free expression of opinion.

The cadet reaction was strongly in favor of the relaxation course and the benefits derived from the training. Ninety-nine per cent reported benefits; 1 per cent were "not interested." Eighty-three per cent reported improvement in ability to go to sleep quickly; 17 per cent did not. Sixty-eight per cent noticed improvement in ability to stay asleep throughout the night; 32 per cent noticed no such improvement. Seventy-seven per cent stated that sleep had become more restful; no improvement was reported by 23 per cent. Seventy-one per cent stated that the

SLEEP CHECK

FOR
- DEL MONTE
- ST. MARYS
- ATHENS

• PARTS
OF BODY
MOVEMENTS

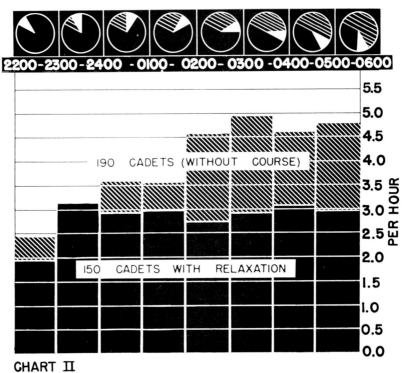

CHART II

relaxation course had helped them in study of academic subjects.

Explanations of the help received were included in their reports. For example, one report stated: "The course has helped me to relax in my studies, especially while taking a test. I do not tense as much when something goes wrong or get excited.[5] In-

---

[5] N.B. This is an example of transient or acute anxiety characteristic in the life of students at school.

SLEEP CHECK

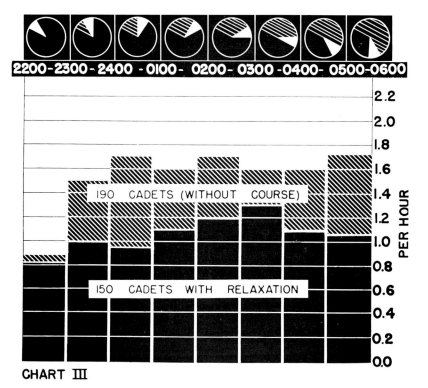

CHART III

stead, I have learned to quietly keep the situation well in hand and also not to make a lot of unnecessary errors in carelessness."

Eighty-five per cent stated that the course had aided them in preparation for examinations and contests. For example, one report stated that the aid received was "by being able to throw off these fears." Sixty-six per cent noted improvement in their athletic performance. Seventy per cent reported that they had been

SLEEP CHECK

FOR
• DEL MONTE
• ST. MARYS
• ATHENS

•TALKING
AND
MUMBLING

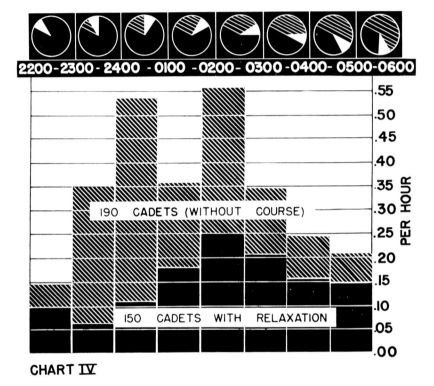

2200-2300-2400-0100-0200-0300-0400-0500-0600

190 CADETS (WITHOUT COURSE)

150 CADETS WITH RELAXATION

PER HOUR

.55
.50
.45
.40
.35
.30
.25
.20
.15
.10
.05
.00

CHART IV

helped in "code, blinker or military." For example, as explained in one report: "The course was . . . good! Really teaches one how to relax in code and blinker. Sitting for long periods, you can relax portions of your body and get up quite refreshed."

Ninety-seven per cent planned to use relaxation methods in flying. Examples of opinions were as follows: "By not using or tensing unnecessary muscles. Believe will tire slower and have

SLEEP CHECK

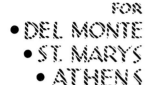

FOR
- DEL MONTE
- ST. MARYS
- ATHENS

• *COMBINING:*
PARTS OF BODY MOVEMENTS..
FULL BODY TURNS...
TALKING AND MUMBLING.

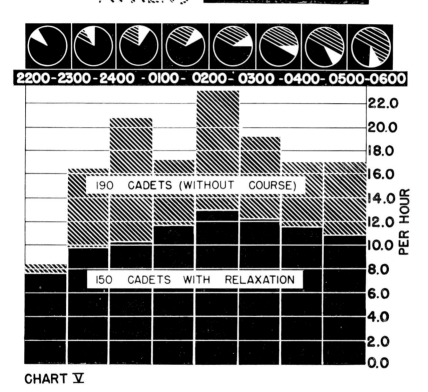

CHART V

better coordination." "For one thing, in check flights you are very likely to get a check pilot who will nag at you and if you can relax, you'll be able to do a better job and not get rattled."

SUMMARY AND CONCLUSIONS

1. In 1943, at United States primary naval training stations, many cadets (perhaps about half) showed symptoms and signs of restlessness, insomnia, fatigue and apprehension. Question-

naires filled out by 3,181 cadets at five preflight schools in their ninth week of training indicated nervous complaints on the part of most of the cadets.

2. Group methods of instruction were employed with the purpose of reducing nervous irritability and excitement in cadets. In preparation, five officers were given a course of instruction in progressive relaxation by Dr. Edmund Jacobson. These officers subsequently instructed other officers, until a total of one hundred relaxation officers became available for instruction of cadets. The cadets were taught progressive relaxation in classes numbering up to three hundred.

3. The course in relaxation for cadets was of ten weeks duration, consisting of three periods per week of one-half hour each. This was an abbreviated course, according to Jacobson's classification, since the total was about ten per cent of the 150 hours of instruction required in a more thorough course. In addition, the cadets generally did not practice with daily regularity as Jacobson prescribes. Accordingly, the following procedures can be regarded as tests of results secured by relaxation methods employed on groups under severe limitations, rather than tests of what could have been accomplished under more satisfactory conditions.

4. Tests at the pre-flight school at Iowa City on 983 cadets who had received such relaxation training indicated approximately 19 per cent reduction of strains, sprains, fractures and other minor injuries in the test group as compared with a control group.

5. Tests on these same groups revealed a 38 per cent reduction of days lost from injuries. Since the control group was considerably smaller than the test group, no quantitative accuracy can be attached to these figures, but they would seem to indicate that, on the whole, a noteworthy reduction of injuries and of days lost from injuries was probably accomplished by the relaxation training.

6. In three preflight schools, data were secured concerning the rest in bed of 140 cadets who had received relaxation training as compared with 190 cadets without training. Marked increase of quietude, recorded in percentages as from twenty-seven to fifty-six, occurred in the number of full body turns, parts of body

movements, and of talking or mumbling. The reports suggested a marked diminution in dreaming. Figures for the total group indicated that the cadets who had received such relaxation training went to sleep more quickly on the whole and suffered less from insomnia during the night.

The data and results reported in this chapter and in the foregoing chapter seem to give practical evidence supporting the general principles of emotion, the thesis of this volume. Applying these principles in medical practice and in educational practice obviously has afforded striking results.

Chapter XIII
RECAPITULATION

IN THE foregoing chapters I have tried to present principles basic to the understanding of emotions and sufficiently sound to prove of service in the practice of medicine. Clinical evidence has been recounted in a monograph entitled *Anxiety and Tension Control*. Further clinical evidence has been related in the present volume, particularly in Chapters XI and XII. Additional evidence will be forthcoming in a volume entitled *Case Histories of Anxiety*. It will be seen that the clinical evidence supports the view of the practical usefulness of the principles herein outlined.

The Welfare Response

In early chapters a unifying response of the behavior patterns of animals on every scale of development was found in the term *welfare response*. Recent studies on the activities of amoebae appear to support the relevancy and the usefulness of the term thus introduced. Review of the many and often brilliant studies on emotional behavior made in various laboratories provide not only a source of vast knowledge, but also likewise appear to confirm the usefulness of the term. This seems the more needed since the countless investigations on the emotions of animals by behavior studies alone and of man by combined objective and subjective methods have led toward a somewhat unordered literature.

Claude Bernard and Walter B. Cannon introduced their well-known conception of homeostasis. This has stimulated an orderly program of research in that important field. It is my hope that, in the still wider field of biology covered by the welfare response, this conception can likewise lead to order and to unified programs of research.

The Free and Independent Life

Homeostasis is indeed a central field in the territory of welfare response. Cannon pointed out that a certain constancy in the internal fluids which bathe the cells constitutes a basic condition for what he called the "free and independent life." Haldane commented that no wiser words were ever uttered by a physiologist.

In higher organisms, free and independent life implies organization in organs, tissues and cells which biologists, including physiologists, have discovered and set forth in countless reports. It includes what Sherrington meant in his famous phrase, "the integrative action of the nervous system." Biologists have found increasing evidence for the integrative action also of enzymes and of hormones, including the integrative action of the entire endocrine system in higher animals. Accordingly, we can speak of the integrating welfare response of the entire human system. From one point of view it is precisely this which apparently is the key to the free and independent life. Support for this view is discussed in the foregoing chapters.

Information Processing

"Information processing" by the nervous system is becoming an outstanding field in present-day physiology. Most of the studies concerned deal with the anatomy and physiology of nerve cells and centers. Nerve impulses are regarded as processes by which internal information is conveyed. Research in this field has opened up a vast field of new knowledge. In current publications, however, emphasis has been chiefly on the anatomical units concerned along with the physicochemical processes.

By Internal Communication

To supplement this, I have tried here to draw attention to the character of the signals of internal communications, since I believe that they are the key to behavior, including emotional behavior.

Nature of Effort

I have tried to point out that the free and independent life consists of innumerable networks of efforts; that effort never occurs excepting upon muscular contraction and relaxation; that with each muscular contraction there is internal communication through the muscle sense, providing one signal of effort, whether consciously received or nearly consciously sensed; that every effort represents physicochemical expenditure of energy; that thus there is a cost as well as an accomplishment in effort.

Animal Behavior is but a Half-Science

We cannot fail to recognize the vast amounts of knowledge which countless investigators have accumulated in the field of emotional behavior in animals. Nevertheless, I have endeavored to point out reasons for believing that the study of emotional behavior in animals is but a half-science, so to speak, since it fails to deal scientifically with the subjective phase of internal signals, the key to behavior. As I have pointed out, sad to relate, many investigators of emotions fail to realize that the subjective senses of man can be studied precisely and with requisite controls just as can be accomplished in other fields of science.

Watson's Doubts

Watson lacked training and experience in this field and showed it by denying the reliability of what he called *introspection.* To be sure, no method becomes scientific until it is adequately understood—until detailed methods are evolved with caution—until proper controls have been elaborated. Skepticism about the reliability of the senses of man often is founded upon whims and caprice rather than upon careful exploration of what these senses can accomplish. Watson evidently never became familiar with the profession of tea tasting, whereby many men make their living and make it possible for corporations engaged in the production and distribution of tea to survive. Watson obviously likewise neglected to consider, or was not familiar with, the variety of sensory observation underlying the wine business of France, including especially the distilled wines of the Cognac district. Without doubt, however, Watson afforded great stimulation to the development of the science of objective observation and recording of emotional behavior.

Lange-James Theory

We reviewed the Lange-James theory of emotion, which William James popularized at the turn of the century. It was dawning upon James that the brain was receiving too much credit in the experience of emotion and that peripheral organs played a role which was neglected. The Lange-James theory emphasized this role. However, these authors suggested that the same stimulus which excited the brain simultaneously excited peripheral organs. Emotion thus was conceived as the result of afferent impulses from the organs reflexly affected. According to this theory, we weep first in time and feel sad later. This theory was sensational but unrealistic. Common experience indicates that we generally feel sad for a brief moment, at least, before we weep.

Theory Never Proved

No carefully conducted and controlled investigations have ever confirmed the belated time relations that were emphasized by the Lange-James theory.

On the contrary, results in the present investigations on emotion conducted over a twenty-year period, the longest on record, have not pointed to any such subsequent occurrence of emotion. On the contrary, all our evidence indicates that the emotional experience is one which depends for its occurrence on circuits simultaneously occurring in the brain and in the neuromuscular system and elsewhere in the organism.

Traditional View of Brain and Mind Lacks Evidence

Accordingly, in Chapter VII, I recited reasons and evidence for believing that brain circuits and neuromuscular circuits operate in simultaneous networks during emotion, the one being as indispensible as the other to a unified and integrated whole. I pointed out that the traditional view that brain action precedes expression in muscles was never supported by laboratory or by clinical evidence based on precise determination of time relations; that brain processes and neuromuscular processes characteristic in emotion are approximately simultaneous in onset and duration.

In popular terms, the traditional view is to the effect that an "idea" is first in the brain and then finds expression in the muscles. According to this view, muscular relaxation, however far it might be carried, would only eliminate peripheral expression, leaving the brain or "mental activity" more or less intact.

Emotion Ceases Upon Advanced Neuromuscular Relaxation

However, in decades of observation with numerous subjects under carefully controlled conditions, I have always found evidence that emotion of any type discontinues when action-potential measurements of muscles show values reduced to the neighborhood of zero. Any emotion at any moment tested is found concurrent with patterns of neuromuscular processes and subsides as these subside. Emotional excitement never has been found present at moments when arm potentials are at zero microvolt levels or in that neighborhood. Most clearly, when eye muscles relax to zero levels or thereabouts, mental activity commonly subsides or becomes absent, including emotion.

Upon sufficiently advanced neuromuscular relaxation, then, no remnant of emotion remains to support the view that the brain can emote independently of the neuromusculature, or that the brain can engage in any other kind of mental activity independently.

Traditional View Is Still Current

We may ask: Why, even today, is there approximately universal acceptance of the traditional view? How has this tradition resisted the advances of electrophysiology and how is it still held true almost universally by scholars? The explanation appears to come from failure to distinguish between the action of individual brain neurones and total brain activity during emotion. Let us consider in intact man impulses proceeding from brain centers efferently to a muscle fiber or to a group with common innervation. Then, in this motor unit, without doubt the efferent discharge in brain and nerves *precedes* the contraction. However, this elementary physiological fact should not be carried over without evidence to the widespread brain action of many neurones which electroencephalography evidences in emotion. Action of one motor unit does not make an emotion, any more than one swallow makes Spring. There is no evidence to support the view that firing of neurones in brain tracts occurs in one volley simultaneously, and that contraction in muscle masses occurs subsequently.

Emotion presumably is not initiated by one neurone but comes into existence upon simultaneous action of many neurones. However, there is every reason to believe that by the time not one but many brain neurons are in operation as a section of the total emotional process, other sections of the emotional process, including particularly the skeletal neuromuscular patterns, are simultaneously in phase. This is nonetheless true, since timing of the psychogalvanic response indicates that the emotion may take several seconds to evolve fully.

How Emotions are Triggered

We engage in unwarranted intellectual abstraction if we assume that an emotion exists apart from other mental activity. In the foregoing pages we have seen evidence that perceptual activity is commonly part and parcel of the emotional pattern. In one sense, as we have seen, emotions are often triggered by vision and visual imagery or by sounds and auditory imagery. However, repetition of such imagery is part and parcel of the emotional experience as the individual attempts an appropriate adjustment, adaptation or welfare response.

Nature of Mental Activity

Here we may briefly recall that, classically, psychologists have striven to resolve all mental activity into three types: (a) sensation; (b) associations; and (c) motion or efferent activity. Herein we leave the classic conception. According to the present thesis, there is no such thing as a sensory or a motor or an associational experience occurring by itself. Every moment of mental activity, on the contrary, is a moment of sensory, of associational and of efferent activity. Thus there is only one variety of mental activity, although in that variety there may be particular emphasis, intensity or duration in one of the three aspects of the activity. So, for example, in pain, the total mental activity or emotional experience accentuates the sensory aspect.

New Principles of Emotion

In Chapter VIII, I presented new principles of emotion based upon x-ray and clinical studies of the spastic digestive tract. Other studies of emotion made in this laboratory or this clinic, not reported upon at length herein, have concerned the cardiovascular system and the respiratory system. In general, the new point of view here presented is that in emotion the individual evaluates the conditions under which he finds himself, including both external and internal conditions.

Evaluation Overlooked

Evaluation is here considered a principle function of emotion, a function which in the past has been neglected. In conditions of emotion when the heartbeat is quickened, this is an element in an organic evaluation of a total situation. When the digestive tract is examined in patients with chronic anxiety states, the esophagus is found to be spastic by the one-swallow test and the colon likewise shows various types of spasticity not only under the x-ray but in other particulars which are characteristic.

Evaluation Is Part of the Welfare Response

The reader will presumably recognize that if emotion is really an attempt at evaluation, this is part and parcel of what has been delineated as the welfare response in Chapters I and II.

Emotion Includes Visceral and Striate Muscle Patterns

Emotion is known to include not only responses of the viscera, appropriate to the situation, as in the case of the classic dogs and cats of Walter Cannon, but also complicated patterns of neuromuscular activity which I have delineated as effort patterns.

Efforts have Purposes

These efforts have a certain measure of purpose. In everyday living we recognize purposeful emotion in a man who is angry, a man who is ashamed, a man who is anxious or otherwise excited. In anger, there is a victim whom he is desirous of moving, or lessening or even of destroying. In love, there is an object of adoration toward which the individual may move if only in caress. In anxiety, there is a problem to be solved. So we might continue with each and every type of emotion. All of this is more or less unconsciously realized in everyday life, although it is scarcely mentioned in the scientific literature.

Emotional Experience Is Part of the Free and Independent Life

However, what has been entirely neglected in past theory and in medical practice is that the participation of skeletal muscles, known by psychologists as voluntary muscles, indicates clearly that emotional experience is part of the free and independent life mentioned above. The neuromuscular patterns which our laboratory investigations not only discover but carefully record and measure in electrical terms are to a large extent, at least, voluntary on the part of the individual. When we move our skeletal muscles in pursuance of an aim, whether emotionally or not, it is an act which we know as voluntary.

To Some Extent Any Emotion Is Voluntary

Insofar as the total emotional pattern is composed of visceral response, we can call the emotion passive or involuntary. However, insofar as the striated musculature participates in complex patterns in each and every emotion, to this extent we can say that the emotion is a part of our voluntary living.

Emotions Not Always for Welfare

Needless to say, although emotions in general often exhibit features of welfare response, this is not always true. Upon listening to music, we often become more or less emotional, yet this scarcely falls into the category of welfare response except with undue extension of the term. Many and various forms of emotion of guilt are not ready to be classified as examples of welfare response. The list could be extended indefinitely. It may even be too much to say that as a rule, emotions are examples of welfare response. Suffice it to say that, in many instances, we can understand the pattern better in the light of the welfare response.

Present Findings Confirmed by Gellhorn

It is well known that emotional excitement tends to diminish objectivity and clarity of reflective thinking. The participation of neuromuscular relaxation, whether cultivated or natural, evidently is indicated where emotional excitement exceeds that conducive to the welfare response. It is of particular interest that Professor Gellhorn has repeated my studies on neuromuscular relaxation in animals and has confirmed the evidence that, with advancing neuromuscular relaxation, emotional excitement decreases.

Control of Emotions Can Be Taught

In Chapter XI were delineated principles for control of human emotions. Clinical evidence was outlined concerning the results attained in controlled clinical investigations. It is found that this is no easy field of teaching endeavor. Patients need to be taught to observe for themselves. Principles and habits of independence of emotion and of action have to be cultivated in them, likewise no easy task for a teacher.

Clinical Results Compared with Psychotherapy

Subject to these limitations, the results attained have greatly exceeded those following any form of psychotherapy, according to the author's experience. This excellence has been recognized by Percival Bailey.[1]

---

[1] BAILEY, P.: The academic lecture: The great psychiatric revolution. *Amer. J. Psychiat., 113,* 5: 397, Nov., 1956.

Emotion Control Taught to U.S. Naval Air Cadets

In Chapter XII was presented evidence that methods of tension control, based upon principles of emotion outlined throughout this text, proved of service in United States Naval Air Cadets suffering from anxiety states while they were learning to fly planes intended for use against the enemy in World War II.

Education for Human Efficiency

It is believed that the principles and practices herein outlined and delineated should be subjected to further controlled investigation. We have seen reasons for believing that cautious educational application of these principles in clinics and in schools and colleges can diminish wear and tear in the human organism as the pathologist uses these terms and, in the words of the engineer, can promote human efficiency.

AUTHOR INDEX

SUBJECT INDEX